THE ROLE OF WATER IN AVOIDING CONFLICT AND BUILDING PROSPERITY

JOINT HEARING

BEFORE THE

SUBCOMMITTEE ON EUROPE, EURASIA, AND EMERGING THREATS

AND THE

SUBCOMMITTEE ON AFRICA, GLOBAL HEALTH, GLOBAL HUMAN RIGHTS, AND INTERNATIONAL ORGANIZATIONS

OF THE

COMMITTEE ON FOREIGN AFFAIRS HOUSE OF REPRESENTATIVES

ONE HUNDRED FOURTEENTH CONGRESS

FIRST SESSION

SEPTEMBER 9, 2015

Serial No. 114–97

Printed for the use of the Committee on Foreign Affairs

Available via the World Wide Web: http://www.foreignaffairs.house.gov/ or http://www.gpo.gov/fdsys/

U.S. GOVERNMENT PUBLISHING OFFICE

96–049PDF   WASHINGTON : 2015

COMMITTEE ON FOREIGN AFFAIRS

EDWARD R. ROYCE, California, *Chairman*

CHRISTOPHER H. SMITH, New Jersey
ILEANA ROS-LEHTINEN, Florida
DANA ROHRABACHER, California
STEVE CHABOT, Ohio
JOE WILSON, South Carolina
MICHAEL T. McCAUL, Texas
TED POE, Texas
MATT SALMON, Arizona
DARRELL E. ISSA, California
TOM MARINO, Pennsylvania
JEFF DUNCAN, South Carolina
MO BROOKS, Alabama
PAUL COOK, California
RANDY K. WEBER SR., Texas
SCOTT PERRY, Pennsylvania
RON DeSANTIS, Florida
MARK MEADOWS, North Carolina
TED S. YOHO, Florida
CURT CLAWSON, Florida
SCOTT DesJARLAIS, Tennessee
REID J. RIBBLE, Wisconsin
DAVID A. TROTT, Michigan
LEE M. ZELDIN, New York
DANIEL DONOVAN, New York

ELIOT L. ENGEL, New York
BRAD SHERMAN, California
GREGORY W. MEEKS, New York
ALBIO SIRES, New Jersey
GERALD E. CONNOLLY, Virginia
THEODORE E. DEUTCH, Florida
BRIAN HIGGINS, New York
KAREN BASS, California
WILLIAM KEATING, Massachusetts
DAVID CICILLINE, Rhode Island
ALAN GRAYSON, Florida
AMI BERA, California
ALAN S. LOWENTHAL, California
GRACE MENG, New York
LOIS FRANKEL, Florida
TULSI GABBARD, Hawaii
JOAQUIN CASTRO, Texas
ROBIN L. KELLY, Illinois
BRENDAN F. BOYLE, Pennsylvania

AMY PORTER, *Chief of Staff*   THOMAS SHEEHY, *Staff Director*
JASON STEINBAUM, *Democratic Staff Director*

SUBCOMMITTEE ON EUROPE, EURASIA, AND EMERGING THREATS

DANA ROHRABACHER, California, *Chairman*

TED POE, Texas
TOM MARINO, Pennsylvania
MO BROOKS, Alabama
PAUL COOK, California
RANDY K. WEBER SR., Texas
REID J. RIBBLE, Wisconsin
DAVID A. TROTT, Michigan

GREGORY W. MEEKS, New York
ALBIO SIRES, New Jersey
THEODORE E. DEUTCH, Florida
WILLIAM KEATING, Massachusetts
LOIS FRANKEL, Florida
TULSI GABBARD, Hawaii

————

SUBCOMMITTEE ON AFRICA, GLOBAL HEALTH, GLOBAL HUMAN RIGHTS, AND INTERNATIONAL ORGANIZATIONS

CHRISTOPHER H. SMITH, New Jersey, *Chairman*

MARK MEADOWS, North Carolina
CURT CLAWSON, Florida
SCOTT DesJARLAIS, Tennessee
DANIEL DONOVAN, New York

KAREN BASS, California
DAVID CICILLINE, Rhode Island
AMI BERA, California

CONTENTS

THE ROLE OF WATER IN AVOIDING CONFLICT AND BUILDING PROSPERITY

WEDNESDAY, SEPTEMBER 9, 2015

House of Representatives,
Subcommittee on Europe, Eurasia, and Emerging Threats and
Subcommittee on Africa, Global Health,
Global Human Rights, and International Organizations,
Committee on Foreign Affairs,
Washington, DC.

The subcommittees met, pursuant to notice, at 2:07 p.m., in room 2172, Rayburn House Office Building, Hon. Dana Rohrabacher (chairman of the Subcommittee on Europe, Eurasia, and Emerging Threats) presiding.

Mr. ROHRABACHER. I call to order this joint hearing of the European, Eurasian, Emerging Threat Subcommittee and the Subcommittee on Africa, Global Health, Global Human Rights, and International Organizations for this afternoon's hearing on issues dealing with clean water, sanitation, and the world.

And I want to thank my fellow members here before I give an opening statement on my part. Thank you both for the contributions you have made to this hearing, but also to this issue over the years. You have both demonstrated such a high level of morality and concern for fellow human beings that will, in and of themselves, those concepts and as part of your soul, will serve our country well in the long run in terms we do what is right. We do what is good for the world in these ways, and make it a better world, it is clearly going to have very positive feedback and blowback on the United States, rather than negative blowback when all we rely on is weapons and trying to get things done by sending troops in the last minute to calm a situation down. So I want to thank you both for your moral and long-term thinking.

Throughout recent hearings, the Europe and Eurasian Subcommittee has explored international water cooperation and discussed examples where water disputes between nations has led to increased tensions. And today we will be discussing water from the point of view of human security.

Access to clean water is absolutely essential to each and every human being. That is why estimates that potentially billions of people in the coming decades will be living in water-stressed areas of the world. So this is a very troubling observation and prediction. Without access to water and the implications that it holds for personal hygiene, agriculture, industry, far too many people will be forced to accept lower standards of living. As Members of Congress concerned with foreign policy, we must think how this dynamic may spark conflicts over natural resources or destabilize very fragile governments.

But this is not only a question for the future. It is a problem of today. This year, we know hundreds of thousands of children will needlessly die from diseases caused by a lack of clean water, plus many more than those hundreds of thousands, many more will die from some disease that can be traced right back to a lack of clean water.

The toll in human suffering caused by a lack of water and dirty water is great, and I am sure witnesses here can explain those stories and how great a problem and challenge that it is.

Yet, I believe the challenges of access to clean water, hygiene, and sanitization can be conquered, and we now have it within our grip, technologically and with the amount of wealth available in our societies, to actually overcome this enormous challenge. Our government through USAID has spent over $3.5 billion over the last decade on programs to do just that; not to mention the efforts of our international partners and nongovernmental organizations.

I believe that as we continue to advance technologically and continue to have innovative ideas that we put into practice, that water scarcity can be managed and mitigated. Increasing human security when it comes to water access and hygiene will not only help improve the lives of these millions of vulnerable people, if not billions of people, but also serve as the strategic interest of the United States. If increasing access to clean water at the micro level helps people in communities to be secure, it follows that their governments will be better able to find solutions to international water disputes.

So without objection, all members will have 5 legislative days to submit additional questions and extraneous material.

But before that, I would like to start off with Mr. Blumenauer or Mr. Smith. Mr. Blumenauer has sort of been our partner on this and several other significant matters.

Mr. Blumenauer, would you enlighten us with an opening statement?

Mr. BLUMENAUER. Mr. Chairman, thank you. Thank you for the courtesy of permitting me to join you and Chairman Smith in this hearing, laying an important foundation. This has been an area of deep personal concern of mine. I have been pleased that in recent Congresses we have been able to get a couple of significant pieces of legislation to focus American foreign policy on water and sanitation. And I would say that there have been no two stronger champions in this bipartisan effort than the two of you. And so I am deeply appreciative of your leadership and your partnership, and it is truly an honor for me to join you.

You laid it out, Mr. Chairman. We have got some certified smart people here who can round out this picture who have been active in recent years. I have had a chance to meet some, and have a new acquaintance here. But the intersection of water, national security, and massive dilemmas in terms of human wellbeing, are significant. There are 261 waterways that cross international boundaries. In some cases, like the Danube, it is 19 countries in the heart of Europe.

An unsettling number of some of the largest rivers in the world no longer flow to the oceans in the course of a year. They are dry for some or all of that period. More than 40 percent of the world's population already lives in an area of physical water scarcity.

And competition is fierce. It is estimated that 20 percent more irrigation water is going to be needed in the next 10 years to keep agriculture going. The Pacific Institute in California has drawn up a list of conflicts in which water has played a part, and they have identified over 200, 204 such incidents where water figured into international conflict. And 61 of those incidents were recent. Looks like the problem is getting more serious, not less.

We have seen it in the Horn of Africa. Part of the chaos in Syria was the result of persistent drought that drove people out of the countryside and into cities where ill-prepared. The situation we are going to be facing in Yemen.

And I would say one area that I look forward to consulting with both of you is to see if we might be able to help focus the United States' efforts in Gaza. No matter what one thinks about the conflict there, we have almost 2 million people who are in an area that the water supply is not going to be, any of it, is going to be fit for human consumption within 2 years. And within less than 5 years, we think that that condition will become permanent. Maybe this is a little area that we could come together to try and deal in a humanitarian sense.

But let me just stop at this point. The National Intelligence Estimate points out that this is a serious issue of national security. You have got some of the best people here. I appreciate your leadership and focus and look forward to being your partner; maybe not on the committee, but maybe as an honorary member of your team. Thank you so very much.

Mr. ROHRABACHER. Mr. Smith.

Mr. SMITH. Thank you very much, Mr. Chairman. And it is indeed an honor to join you, Chairman Rohrabacher, and I thank you for your leadership on this extremely important issue.

And, Mr. Blumenauer, it is a delight to be with you again, and thank you for your legislation, which did become law, which I think is a landmark piece of legislation. It was very bipartisan, but you walked point, and I thank you for that extraordinary leadership as well.

Like you, Mr. Chairman, my subcommittee has had and held several hearings on health and water, and it is clear that without adequate supplies of clean drinking water and proper sanitation no health programming can succeed. Indeed, the World Health Organization estimates that because of a lack of access to safe drinking water and sanitation, more than 14,000 people die daily from water-borne illnesses which cause more than 1 billion cases of intestinal worms, 1.4 million child deaths each year from diarrhea, 860,000 child deaths each year from malnutrition, and 500,000 deaths from all age groups each year from malaria.

I note parenthetically that I have introduced legislation that we are really pushing hard to enact about neglected tropical diseases, and it would really take that whole issue to a new realm of prioritization and backing. But, again, without water, and without trying to address water needs, all of those efforts are stymied. And of course, that is integrated into our bill.

It is troubling that so many people in the world do not have ready access to water. The U.N. has estimated 2.6 billion people have gained access to safe drinking water over the last 25 years, but another 663 million continue to lack access as of this year. Nearly half of these people live in Africa, another fifth live in South Asia.

As we know, the U.N. Millennium Development Goals, the MDGs, included a target for access to safe drinking water and basic sanitation. According to the U.N., global goals for access for water are being met, but sanitation continues to be unmet. Of course, that is defined as having globally the proportion of people who are without sustainable access to safe drinking water and basic sanitation. So it is a movement in the right direction, but certainly not an achievement of universal access.

Over the past 10 years, the U.S. Government has spent $3.5 billion on water, sanitation, and hygiene, or WASH programming. Nevertheless, even after several water acts passed by Congress and great international effort to bring countries up to global WASH standards, U.S. programming still remains somewhat disjointed. According to the GAO study just being concluded, there is no uniform model that has been created for WASH programming. USAID was supposed to present a comprehensive plan for WASH programming this year, but none has been released as of this time.

Even if a model program were to be made adaptable to each country, by now there should be some overall strategy for how to design a program, monitor its progress, and evaluate its outcomes. In too many countries in which USAID operates WASH programs, there is no comprehensive program. Monitoring is limited and evaluation fails to adequately assess the statistics being provided by host governments.

The human cost of failure to provide adequate WASH programming is too high to allow substandard programming to continue. We will hear that there has been progress made, and this is indeed promising, but there is more that must be done. And, again, we have the experts here today to provide a road map to our committees as to how we should proceed.

I thank you, Mr. Chairman.

Mr. ROHRABACHER. Thank you very much.

Now we have three witnesses. I will be introducing the three of them. We will have testimony, and then we will have questions and answers for all three witnesses at the same time.

Let me suggest to the witnesses, if you can summarize in 5 minutes, that would be great and give us more time to have a bit of a dialogue on this.

We have three wonderful witnesses, as I say. John Oldfield is the CEO of WASH Advocates. And I am trying to guess, you have Water and Sanitation Health?

Mr. OLDFIELD. Hygiene.

Mr. ROHRABACHER. Hygiene.

Mr. OLDFIELD. Hygiene. Health is a good guess, though.

Mr. ROHRABACHER. Okay, there we go—WASH advocates, an organization dedicated to increasing the awareness of global WASH challenges and solutions. Previously, he founded two implementing nonprofit organizations and was with the National Academy of Sciences, where he researched science and technology policy.

And next we have from my home county Denis Bilodeau, who is the vice president of the Orange County Water District, and was elected to his fourth term in 2012. He is a licensed civil and traffic engineer, holds a bachelor degree in civil engineering from the University of California at Irvine.

And let me just note that we in Orange County are proud that we have what we believe is the most technologically sophisticated and up-to-date water system in the world. And we will let him describe that and the implications of that for these various countries that are facing a serious challenge.

Dale Wittington is a professor at the University of North Carolina at Chapel Hill in the Department of Environmental Science and Engineering, and City and Regional Planning. He is a member of the Technological Committee on the Global Water Partnership and has served as consultant on water and sanitation policies to the World Bank, USAID, and numerous other organizations.

So we have some very, like I say, witnesses that are very impressive with their credentials.

And may we proceed, Mr. Oldfield?

STATEMENT OF MR. JOHN OLDFIELD, CHIEF EXECUTIVE OFFICER, WASH ADVOCATES

Mr. OLDFIELD. Thank you, Mr. Chairman. I was pretty proud of my opening remarks here until I heard yours. It is going to be hard to beat that. I am gratified that some of the certified smart people are up there as well. So thank you for yours.

Thank you, Chairman Rohrabacher, Chairman Smith, Ranking Member Meeks, Ranking Member Bass, and distinguished members, Mr. Blumenauer, for the opportunity to provide these brief remarks, which are a summary of my written statement.

Thank you, before I begin, for your interest and your support for safe drinking water, sanitation, and hygiene programs throughout Africa, Asia, and Latin America over the last at least decade.

I also, before I continue, want to recognize and in fact applaud the U.S. civic organizations, religious groups, student clubs, corporations, academics, private philanthropists, nonprofits, and then my fellow panelists, my fellow witnesses, who are all working to solve this challenge with us today.

Safe drinking water, sanitation, and hygiene are about, its most simple terms, about the dignity and personal and economic security of human beings. A life without WASH is a very difficult one. You may remember a situation 2 years ago where two young women were raped and murdered in Uttar Predesh, India, raped and murdered on the way to go to the bathroom in a field at night. That story actually, I think, helped galvanize Congress to support the Water for the World Act that was referenced and to strengthen appropriations language, so thank you again for that.

And as I was preparing this testimony, I also learned of an extraordinarily sad situation from my friends at Special Olympics in Nigeria. A 15-year-old girl with an intellectual disability was raped on her way to fetch water from a local river for her school, a state school for students with intellectual disabilities in southern Nigeria. Now, that girl, a Special Olympics athlete, faces challenges in life that most of us can hardly imagine, and a lack of safe drinking water should not be one of them.

In both of these situations there were larger societal challenges involved, but if these women had safe drinking water and a private, safe place to go to the bathroom their lives would undoubtedly be or have been more secure and more productive.

Now, beyond these painful stories, there are hundreds of millions of women who spend far too much of their time and far too much of their income acquiring, as you have stated, just enough water to keep themselves and their families alive, if not actually healthy, on a daily basis. In 2015, hundreds of millions of women and girls are wasting their lives carrying water. Imagine what would each of us do if we had an extra 3 or 4 hours a day, how much more secure would we feel, how much more economically productive would we be?

This is solvable. I think all three of you have said that. And Congress has been a key ally for well over a decade here. The Water for the Poor Act of 2005, of course, made safe drinking water, sanitation, and hygiene a priority of U.S. foreign policy. The Water for the World Act of 2014 further directs USAID to make WASH investments with the biggest contributions to global public health, alongside improved monitoring and evaluation, enhanced accountability, and decentralized ownership.

This year, House appropriators reasserted congressional intent to prioritize WASH and its fundamental contributions to health and to the security of the world's poorest people. The appropriators wrote: "Access to adequate water, sanitation, and hygiene is a critical component of disease prevention, and a lack of access to toilets and adequate sanitation impacts women and girls in particular."

The global WASH challenge is both an emerging threat and an emerging opportunity. For 10 years, Congress and both the Bush and the Obama administrations have provided bipartisan support, moving WASH efforts to what I considered to be the leading edge of foreign assistance reform by focusing on strengthening local capacity and increasing accountability across Africa, Asia, and Latin America.

However, Congress can further improve human and economic security across the developing world and should, A, continue to provide strong oversight of these issues; B, increase the amount, the effectiveness, and the targeting of annual appropriations; C, seek additional leverage for U.S. taxpayer dollars through additional partnerships and innovative finance; D, make WASH a more prominent piece of our bilateral relationships with many countries; and E, prioritize water and sanitation first of all as an important sector in its own right, but secondly, as the foundation of long-lasting progress toward public health, conflict prevention, undernutrition, and economic development.

Now, years ago an early supporter of the Water for the Poor Act that became law in 2005 said: "It is the human condition that must be improved if national security is to be strengthened." You might recall that quote. Sitting here today, I see no better way to improve the human condition than by providing safe drinking water, sanitization, and hygiene to more families and communities across the globe. And I and many, many others are grateful for your continuing support. Thank you.

[The prepared statement of Mr. Oldfield follows:]

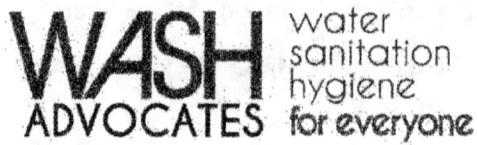

House Committee on Foreign Affairs

Subcommittee on Europe, Eurasia, and Emerging Threats

Subcommittee on Africa, Global Health, Global Human Rights, and
International Organizations

The Role of Water in Avoiding Conflict and Building Prosperity

September 9, 2015

Testimony by:

John Oldfield, CEO

WASH Advocates
Safe Drinking Water, Sanitation, and Hygiene for All

Thank you Chairman Rohrabacher, Chairman Smith, Ranking Member Meeks, Ranking
Member Bass and distinguished members of the Subcommittees for the opportunity to
provide these brief remarks.

On behalf of WASH Advocates, our many partners, and millions of people across the globe,
let me first thank you for your interest and support for safe drinking water, sanitation, and
hygiene (WASH) programs throughout Africa, Asia, and Latin America over the years. I also
want to recognize and applaud the many American citizens helping meet this challenge.
Thousands of civic organizations, churches and other religious groups, student clubs,
corporations, academics, private philanthropies, and nonprofits are doing more every year
to solve this challenge, frequently in partnership with the U.S. government. And it's
working.

Summary

The global safe drinking water and sanitation challenge is both an emerging threat and an
emerging opportunity for the U.S. government and private Americans from all 50 states. By
continuing to support safe drinking water, sanitation, and hygiene (WASH) as a priority of
U.S. foreign policy, Congress has an opportunity to improve human and economic security
across Africa, Asia, and Latin America. Since the passage of the Water for the Poor Act in
2005, both Congress and the Bush and Obama Administrations have provided important
support for this issue in a nonpartisan and increasingly effective manner, positioning safe
drinking water and sanitation efforts at the leading edge of foreign assistance reform by

focusing on strengthening local capacity and increasing accountability. Congress has a clear opportunity to build on this momentum, and should:

a) continue to provide strong oversight,
b) increase the amount, effectiveness, and targeting of annual appropriations,
c) seek additional leverage for U.S. taxpayer dollars through additional partnerships and innovative finance,
d) make WASH a more prominent piece of our bilateral relationships, and
e) prioritize water and sanitation as an important sector in its own right and as the foundation of longterm progress toward other related development challenges including public health, conflict prevention and mitigation, food security and under-nutrition, gender empowerment, and economic development.

Introduction

I applaud your Subcommittees' interest and support for global water issues over the past couple of years, particularly for your focus on water as a component of conflict and on the linkages between water, sanitation, and health. Your efforts – and those of your colleagues and collaborators inside the Beltway and far beyond – are saving and improving millions of lives across the globe. I would also like to recognize and applaud the commitment and efforts of the other witnesses from the University of North Carolina and the Orange County Water District for their work toward solutions to the global water challenge.

Safe drinking water, sanitation, and hygiene are about the dignity and personal and economic security of human life. A life without WASH is a very difficult one. As I was preparing this testimony, I learned of an extraordinarily sad situation from my friends at Special Olympics in Nigeria. A 15 year old young woman with an intellectual disability was raped on her way to fetch water from a local river for her school, a state school for persons with intellectual disabilities in southern Nigeria. This young woman – a Special Olympics athlete – faces challenges in life that most of us can hardly imagine, and a lack of safe drinking water should not be one of them.

And I also thought back to the all-too-common tragedy two years ago in Uttar Pradesh, India, where two young women were raped and murdered on their way to go to the bathroom in a field. These two young women lived very challenging, if brief, lives, and a lack of a proper, private place to go to the bathroom should not have been one of those challenges.

A lack of safe drinking water and a lack of proper sanitation facilities are certainly not the sole causes of these two incidents. There are larger, societal challenges involved in both cases, but if these women and their communities had safe drinking water and sanitation, their lives would undoubtedly be – or have been – more secure and productive.

One particular Member of Congress from the House Foreign Affairs Committee has been one of the strongest champions of the linkages between WASH and women across the globe. A brief quote from one of his recent speeches:

> *[This] is a victims issue and here's why... in parts of the world women spend the whole day – the whole day – seeking clean water.... That doesn't allow them to do other things that they need to do in their families because they spend so much time travelling. And when they usually take their small kids – girls in many cases – to some area to just get a little water, they are met with some bad guys – just waiting there, not doing anything, just waiting for prey. They (the bad guys) control the water system (well, creek), and for that lady to have access to a little fresh water, they do bad things to her...*
>
> *... that should not occur anywhere in the world. It gets my blood pressure up and it oughta get yours up... We have it within our power to stop that and make sure that woman and her family have access to clean water.*
>
> *We should do what we need to do as a nation to solve these problems.*

Thank you, Congressman Poe, for your ongoing, deeply personal commitment to these challenges, and for showing with your work with Congressman Earl Blumenauer of Oregon and many others that politics does indeed stop at water.

It's not just these headline-grabbing, horrific stories that should hold our attention. There are hundreds of millions of women across the globe who spend an inordinate amount of their time, and tens of millions of families who spend an unreasonable amount of their income, acquiring enough water (often of poor quality) to keep them alive – if not healthy – through each day. It's 2015, and hundreds of millions of women and girls are being used as pipes – as water and even wastewater infrastructure. Hundreds of millions of women and girls have to deal with localized violence, crime, and conflict, in their search for water and a safe place to go the bathroom.

We in the U.S. have thankfully not lived under these conditions for some time, but hundreds of millions of people around the globe face this reality every single day. If freedom from fear is human security, and freedom from want is economic security, there are currently billions of people who are living insecure lives.

As evidenced over the past decade by the Water for the Poor Act of 2005, the Water for the World Act of 2014, and by statutory and report language in appropriations bills, Congress has understood the fundamental nature of this challenge for some time. The Water for the Poor Act of 2005 first made safe drinking water and sanitation a priority of U.S. foreign policy. The Water for the World Act of 2014 further focuses the Administration's efforts

primarily on the linkages between water, sanitation, and human health across the developing world. FY16 recommended report language also makes clear the House of Representatives' interest in the contributions that WASH makes to public health and to making the lives of women more secure:

> "*Access to adequate water, sanitation, and hygiene is a critical component of disease prevention...*" and "*The Committee notes that a lack of access to toilets and adequate sanitation impacts women and girls in particular and recommends USAID work to ensure this issue is addressed in the design of WASH programs.*"

The good news: this is solvable. The tools exist across the globe to ensure that children, women, and families will soon have the safe drinking water, sanitation, and hygiene that they need to live more secure lives. The tools exist so that instead of water managing women, women will now manage water. The tools exist so that families do not have to pay a disproportionate part of their daily income for safe drinking water. The tools exist to strengthen the dialogues between citizens and their governments across the globe, using water as a step toward more open, democratic societies. The tools exist to allow girl students to carry schoolbooks, not water, on their heads every morning.

A very brief list of just some of these tools includes:
- properly constructed wells and piping systems so that women are no longer used as infrastructure
- rainwater harvesting systems to get families through the dry season so that the next drought does not become the next famine
- latrines and other sanitation facilities that properly capture and dispose of human waste to reduce the transmission of often fatal diarrheal disease, including cholera
- WASH in Schools – single gender school toilets and menstrual hygiene products made by local organizations with locally available material, e.g. banana fiber – to increase enrollment and retention
- programs to strengthen the management of water and wastewater utilities across the globe
- small businesswomen making and selling bars of soap wrapped in hygiene messages to their neighbors (handwashing with soap can reduce diarrheal disease transmission by up to 47%[1]),
- providing WASH in hospitals and other health care facilities as a means to reduce infectious diseases, strengthen health systems, and/or prevent the next Ebola, cholera, or other disease outbreak; this is a vital linkage that many stakeholders (WHO, Global Health Council, WaterAid, members of the Millennium Water Alliance) are pursuing aggressively

---

[1] Curtis, V. & Cairncross, S. (2003). Effect of washing hands with soap on diarrhoea risk in the community: a systematic review. *The Lancet Infectious Diseases.* 3(5), 275-281.

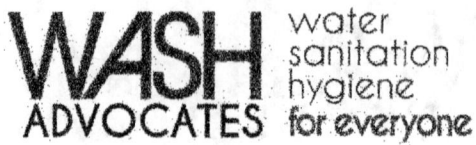

- governments and private sector stakeholders across the globe inventing and commercializing new ways to properly treat human waste and turn it into biogas and fertilizer to both minimize the effects of large amounts of human waste being released into the environment and maximize the economic upside of that waste
- properly functioning community water associations managing their own water and sanitation services with no assistance from any international donor; a women's first experience with participatory democracy may often be her village water committee, and the Avina Foundation, a private philanthropist, and World Justice Project, a U.S. nonprofit, are making those linkages more clear.

The best news: this is being solved. Households, communities, their governments and private sector allies are solving these problems every hour of every day across Africa, Asia, and Latin America. The numbers are improving. The international donor community, in many cases led by the United States, is helping, and I believe can do more and better. Americans are already providing these basic services to millions across the globe. In the most recent report from USAID on the implementation of its Water and Development Strategy, USAID notes that in FY 2014 more than 3.2 million people gained access to improved drinking water supply, and nearly 1.9 million people gained access to improved sanitation facilities. A particularly salient quote from former USAID Administrator Raj Shah opens the report:

> "Development is a fundamental part of our national security. It is extreme poverty – the realities of access to water and food – which creates the long-term drivers of our insecurity."

Background

WASH Advocates is a nonprofit education and advocacy effort entirely dedicated to solving the global safe drinking water, sanitation, and hygiene (WASH) challenge. We have been fully funded for our work since 2005 by a small group of private philanthropists that have included the Conrad N. Hilton Foundation, the Wallace Genetic Foundation, the Howard G. Buffett Foundation, the Laird Norton Family Foundation, the Osprey Foundation, and others. We receive no federal funding. Our mission is simply to increase both the amount and effectiveness of U.S. funding and programming in the global WASH sector.

Water and Conflict

You have tasked your witnesses today with illustrating the linkages between water, avoiding conflict, and building economic prosperity. I have reviewed many of the two Subcommittees' recent hearings on water, geopolitical threats, and global health.

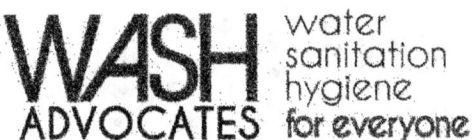

You also will recall that the U.S. intelligence community in 2012, via its *"Intelligence Community Assessment on Global Water Security[2]*," and the classified version to which you have access, identified water as a potential source of significant security challenges to this country and our allies over the next decade. The intelligence report also found that the U.S. is well positioned to help respond to these challenges, and expected by our allies to respond.

Today I would like to address a highly localized type of conflict: the conflict and physical and economic insecurity that hundreds of millions of women and families must deal with on a daily basis around the world because of a lack of safe drinking water or a safe place to go the bathroom. As Administrator Shah said, and as the Members of these Subcommittees understand, these are the conditions that create the *"long-term drivers of our insecurity."*

It sounds quite intuitive, and there are many anecdotes showing the linkages between WASH and localized violence, including gender-based violence, but this field of study is just beginning to emerge. In preparing this testimony, I found the examples below demonstrate well the linkages between water and localized conflict:

1) PLAN, WaterAid, CARE and others contributed to a 62 page document[3] filled with case studies that show as clearly as possible the links between WASH and various forms of violence, mostly gender-based:
    a. sexual violence (rape, assault)
    b. psychological violence (harassment, bullying)
    c. physical violence (beating, fighting)
    d. social-cultural violence (discrimination, political marginalization)

    This is an extraordinarily difficult document to read but hopefully will lead to many of its promising good practices being adopted across the globe.

2) Dr. Robert Dreibelbis, Assistant Professor from the University of Oklahoma, writes *"....there is a link between WASH access and conflict and violence. However, we are only now beginning to document and quantify this association. We do know that this association is much more complicated than just having access to infrastructure - poorly designed, poorly positioned, and poorly managed infrastructure can often compound and/or magnify violence and conflict. Further, the link between WASH and violence is inherently bound within broader systems of gender inequities."* One of the studies he sent me details a study of women and sanitation in India[4]. It states in part *"... women encountered three broad types of stressors - environmental, social, and sexual - the intensity of which were modified by the woman's life stage, living environment, and access to sanitation facilities. Environmental barriers, social factors*

---

[2] Office of the Director of National Intelligence (2012). *Global Water Security – Intelligence Community Assessment.* Retrieved from the US Department of State website: http://www.state.gov/e/oes/water/ica
[3] http://violence-wash.lboro.ac.uk
[4] http://www.sciencedirect.com/science/article/pii/S0277953615300010

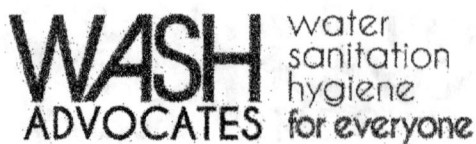

and fears of sexual violence all contributed to sanitation-related psychosocial stress. Though women responded with small changes to sanitation practices, they were unable to significantly modify their circumstances, notably by achieving adequate privacy for sanitation-related behaviors. . . "

3) I would also direct the Subcommittees' attention to USAID's *"Water & Conflict: A Toolkit for Programming,[5]"* which begins with *"Water is an essential ingredient for human security* [i.e. security for the individual, not the state] *and sustainable development,"* and then states *". . . disputes over water, whether scarce or abundant, do not always result in violence. In fact, the management of water often brings parties together and encourages cooperation; it can be an integral factor in conflict prevention, peacebuilding, and reconciliation processes. Since fresh water is irreplaceable and indispensable to life, it is a valuable and contested resource that requires careful, conflict-sensitive management to ensure that it will continue to fulfill its purposes over the long term."* Many of the Program Options within the document focus on various ways to strengthen dialogues between citizens and their public officials to stay ahead of potential conflict due to water- and sanitation-related challenges.

4) There are myriad other examples of where water and sanitation are being developed in part to prevent or mitigate localized conflict. Those examples come from across northern and sub-Saharan Africa, South and Southeast Asia, and Central and South America, and from organizations such as Catholic Relief Services, Millennium Water Alliance, CARE, International Rescue Committee, and more, many of whom are USAID partners. One of the most compelling is a gravity-fed water system (funded by USAID, and implemented by CARE and local partners) with ten water points contributing to both peace and stronger market opportunities between Muslim pastoralists selling livestock and Christian agriculturalists selling cereal crops in Ethiopia.

Inadequate water and sanitation multiply, magnify, and accelerate related threats across the development spectrum. However, if we look at water and sanitation more as an "emerging opportunity" than as an "emerging threat" we find WASH makes significant contributions to public health (including HIV/AIDS and Neglected Tropical Diseases), primary and secondary education, opportunities for girls and women, food security and under-nutrition, poverty alleviation, and others. This is an emerging threat that is also clearly an emerging leadership opportunity. WASH also contributes heavily to the prevention and mitigation of the next disease outbreak (e.g., Ebola or cholera), and to strengthening healthcare facilities and systems across the globe. Long-term success with these related development priorities is more likely if those initiatives are built on a secure foundation of safe drinking water and sanitation. And the reverse also holds true: without

[5] USAID (2014). *Water & Conflict: A Tool for Programming.* Retrieved from USAID website: https://www.usaid.gov/sites/default/files/documents/1866/WaterConflictToolkit.pdf

water and sanitation, long-term progress toward these other development objectives will likely be stunted.

The global water, sanitation, and hygiene challenge is grave. An estimated 663 million people currently live without safe drinking water, and 2.4 billion live without sanitation – without a safe place to go to the bathroom[6]. Many of the best minds in the WASH sector anticipate that those numbers are low as they insufficiently include water quality measures, and infrastructure resilience metrics. This lack of safe drinking water and sanitation sickens, stunts the physical and cognitive development of, and reduces the economic productivity of billions, and kills millions, including a significant number of children under five years of age.

WASH and Economic Prosperity

Safe drinking water, sanitation, and hygiene (WASH) help children, families, communities and economies survive and thrive throughout the developed and developing world. The challenges associated with unsafe water and sanitation are grave but solvable. The key is getting the solutions to where they are most needed.

And it is important that it be solved: above and beyond the lives that safe drinking water saves and improves, every dollar invested in water and sanitation in developing countries returns at least $4 for that $1 investment[7]. This return comes primarily in the form of increased economic productivity (time savings) and decreased healthcare costs. Imagine what each of us could do with an extra four to six hours each day not spent hauling water around on our heads. You will hear more about this from Dr. Whittington of the University of North Carolina, but a couple of quick data points follow.

The World Bank's Water and Sanitation Program leads an effort called the Economics of Sanitation Initiative. Its first study – in 2007 – found that *"the economic costs of poor sanitation and hygiene amounted to over US$9.2 billion a year (2005 prices) in Cambodia, Indonesia, Lao PDR, the Philippines, and Vietnam. The groundbreaking study was the first of its kind to attribute dollar amounts to a country's losses from poor sanitation. The report sparked public awareness and Government action in several countries.[8]"* A related study in Africa indicated that *"eighteen African countries lose around US$5.5 billion every year due to*

[6] WHO/UNICEF (2015). *Progress on Sanitation and Drinking Water – 2015 Update and MDG Assessment.* Retrieved from WHO/UNICEF Joint Monitoring Programme (JMP) for Water and Sanitation website: http://www.wssinfo.org/fileadmin/user_upload/resources/JMP-Update-report-2015_English.pdf

[7] WHO. (2012). *Global costs and benefits of drinking-water supply and sanitation interventions to reach the MDG target and universal coverage.* Retrieved from the WHO website: www.who.int/water_sanitation_health/publications/2012/globalcosts.pdf

[8] Hutton G, Rodriguez UE, Napitupulu L, Thang P, Kov P. (2008). *Economic impacts of sanitation in Southeast Asia.* World Bank, Water and Sanitation Program. Retrieved from the World Bank website: http://www.wsp.org/sites/wsp.org/files/publications/Sanitation_Impact_Synthesis_2.pdf

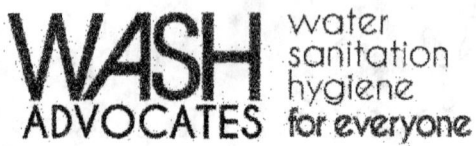

poor sanitation, with annual economic losses between 1% and 2.5% of GDP.[9]" And in India:
"The total economic impacts of inadequate sanitation in India amount[ed] to a loss of $ 53.8 billion in 2006. These economic impacts were the equivalent of about 6.4% of India's gross domestic product (GDP) in 2006.[10]"

These studies are becoming dated, and the good news is that sanitation coverage has increased in coverage since they were done, likely leading to reduced economic impacts of inadequate sanitation.

Another way to approach the linkages between water and economic prosperity is to take a look at new business and financial models underway in the sector. Water.org, a U.S. nonprofit led by Gary White, who is on WASH Advocates' Global Advisory Council, is building microcredit facilities in the WASH sector in India and elsewhere. A woman in Bangalore, India was paying approximately $0.70/day (40 rupees) for water and sanitation services for her family, a significant portion of the family's income. Her payments for a WaterCredit loan for a toilet and water connection for her home are the same as what she was accustomed to paying for water and sanitation previously. However, once that loan is paid off (two years), her family's income will increase significantly, even after she pays for the ongoing maintenance for the water and sanitation services. Water.org writes "WaterCredit is boosting family income, and boosting how much time women have. Women are now able to invest more in other family health issues. It elevates the economic standing of the person taking out the loan, and it preserves charity for those most in need." Water.org also has significant such work underway in India in collaboration with the PepsiCo Foundation and its local financial partners.

Another prominent U.S. nonprofit, PSI, is working with USAID to jumpstart WASH markets, creating jobs for sanitation and water providers in Ghana, Benin, Cote d'Ivoire, and Senegal, creating more business opportunities for WASH entrepreneurs and growing these economies.

The Water Supply and Sanitation Collaborative Council's Global Sanitation Fund in Senegal has been using handwashing to empower women and generate income. One of their programs trained women to make and sell soap, increasing their personal income and generating significant health benefits.[11]

---

[9] World Bank Water and Sanitation Program (2012). Retrieved from World Bank website: https://www.wsp.org/content/africa-economic-impacts-sanitation

[10] Tyagi, A. (2011). *Economic impacts of inadequate sanitation in India*. World Bank Water and Sanitation Program. Retrieved from the World Bank website: http://www.wsp.org/sites/wsp.org/files/publications/WSP-esi-india.pdf

[11] https://wsscafricasan4.wordpress.com/2015/05/27/engaging-communities-in-matam-senegal/

Highlights relevant to the WASH / economic prosperity nexus from USAID's recent Safeguarding the World's Water report[12] include:

- Through USAID's Development Innovation Ventures, Sanergy is building 700 toilets that will serve 90,000 residents of Kenya's informal settlements. Sanergy franchises toilets to residents of these settlements who collect the waste from the toilets and convert it to nutrient-rich organic fertilizer; the operators create a profit of up to $2,000/year.
- USAID's Sustainable Water & Sanitation in Africa (SUWASA) works to promote commercial solutions and financial sustainability for the water and sanitation sectors in the urban areas of sub-Saharan Africa. In Kenya, SUWASA worked with local banks and utilities to mobilize previously unavailable local private finance. Improvements in the financial sector reduce aid dependence and can fundamentally change the way water and wastewater utilities work.
- The Tanzania Integrated Water, Sanitation, and Hygiene (iWASH) Program supports the delivery of sustainable, market-driven WASH services to improve health and increase economic resiliency of the poor. iWASH is part of USAID's Global Water for Sustainability program and receives support from the Water and Development Alliance, a public-private partnership between USAID and the Coca-Cola Foundation. In FY 2013, iWASH brought first-time access to clean, safe drinking water to more than 53,500 people, over 50 percent of whom were women or girls. The program also provided hygiene and sanitation education to close to 64,000 people and access to improved sanitation facilities to over 11,500 people, mostly through the construction and rehabilitation of school latrines.

<u>Integrating WASH and Other Development Sectors</u>

WASH is its own important development sector, and has positive, corollary impacts on related development objectives:

WASH and Health:
- Diarrhea is one of the leading causes of child death in the world today, and is predominantly caused by poor sanitation, hygiene, or dirty drinking water.[13]
- Simple handwashing, an element of hygiene programming, can reduce the incidence of childhood respiratory infections, such as pneumonia, by at least 23%,[14] and

[12] USAID (2015). *Safeguarding the World's Water: Report for USAID Fiscal Year 2014 Water Sector Activities.* Retrieved from USAID website: https://www.usaid.gov/documents/1865/safeguarding-world's-water
[13] WHO, *Safer Water, Better Health: Costs, Benefits and Sustainability to Interventions to Protect and Promote Health,* 2008
[14] Rabie T and Curtis V (2006) "Handwashing and risk of respiratory infections: a quantitative systematic review" in *Tropical Medicine and International Health,* 11(3), 258-267.

diarrheal disease by approximately 45%.[15] Awareness of the health benefits of handwashing is still low in many poor communities.

- People living with HIV/AIDS and others with compromised immune systems, are more prone to common illnesses and diseases such as diarrhea. As such, access to improved sanitation and water supply is essential to the overall health of people living with HIV/AIDS.[16]
- Adequate nutrition—compromised by diarrhea, which reduces the body's retention of nutrients—is fundamental for people taking antiretroviral drugs. Water and sanitation can improve the efficacy of the significant U.S. investment in HIV/AIDS treatment. One study of people living with HIV/AIDS in Uganda found that the presence of a latrine reduced the risk of diarrheal disease by 31%.[17]
- WASH and Neglected Tropical Diseases (NTDs): Chairman Smith, at a hearing two years ago, stated: "Generally, Neglected Tropical Diseases affect the health of the poor in developing countries where access to clean water, sanitation and healthcare is limited." Congressional colleagues are listening, and FY16 recommended appropriations report language from the House includes: "*Access to adequate water, sanitation, and hygiene is a critical component of disease prevention, and the Committee directs the USAID Administrator to consult with the Committees on Appropriations on its efforts to incorporate the goal of clean water across health and development programs.*"
- "In low resource settings, WASH services in many healthcare facilities are absent. Data from 54 countries, representing 66,101 facilities show that, 38% of health care facilities do not have an improved water source, 19% do not have improved sanitation and 35% do not have water and soap for handwashing. This lack of services compromises the ability to provide basic, routine services, such as child delivery and compromises the ability to prevent and control infections."[18]
- "For those living in rural areas, primary health care facilities are frequently the first point of care. As such, these facilities play a critical role in maternal and newborn health, and in responding to disease outbreaks, such as cholera or Ebola. Yet, without WASH, the ability of health care workers to carry out proper infection prevention and control measures and demonstrate to communities safe WASH

---

[15] Curtis V and Cairncross S. Effect of washing hands with soap on diarrhoea risk in the community: a systematic review. *The Lancet Infectious Diseases* 2003; 3:275-281.

[16] Obi, CL, B. Onabolu, M.N.B. Momba, J.O. Igumbor, J. Ramalivahna, P.O. Bessong, E.J. van Rensburg, M. Lukoto, E. Green, and T.B. Mulaudzi. The interesting cross-paths of HIV/AIDS and water in Southern Africa with special reference to South Africa. South African Water Research Commission, Vol. 32 No. 3, July 2006.

[17] Weinger, Merri. Dignity for All: Sanitation, Hygiene and HIV/AIDS. USAID, 2008

[18] WHO/UNICEF (2015). *Water, sanitation and hygiene in health care facilities: Status in low- and middle-income countries and way forward.* Retrieved from WHO website: http://www.who.int/water_sanitation_health/publications/wash-health-care-facilities/en

practices is greatly compromised."[19] These are vital linkages that many stakeholders (WHO, Global Health Council, WaterAid) are pursuing now – and key to preventing or reducing the severity of the next Ebola, cholera, or other infectious disease outbreak.

We encourage the water team at USAID to continue its efforts to work with its agency counterparts in global health to position water and sanitation as a means toward meeting public health objectives across the developing world, reducing the need for additional humanitarian assistance.

WASH and Women: Surveys from 45 developing countries show that women and children bear the primary responsibility for water collection in the vast majority of households. This is time not spent generating income, caring for family members, or attending school, and as I mentioned earlier often leads to physical security threats to these women and girls.[20] The World Health Organization estimates that women and children spend 140 million hours each day collecting water.[21]

WASH, Under-Nutrition, and Food Security: Malnutrition and diarrheal disease are closely linked. When it doesn't kill, repeated bouts of early childhood diarrhea can negatively impact physical and cognitive development.[22] Reductions in diarrheal disease, which could be achieved by providing improved sanitation and water supply, can prevent long term morbidity and at least 860,000 child deaths a year caused by malnutrition.[23]

We also encourage the water team at USAID to continue to strengthen their partnership with ongoing nutrition and food security efforts. This collaboration, as outlined in USAID's Water and Development Strategy and USAID's Multi-sectoral Nutrition Strategy 2014-2025[24], should include efforts focused both on water in agriculture and on efforts to make sure that people in Africa, Asia, and Latin America have the safe drinking water they need

---

[19] WHO/UNICEF (2015). *Water, sanitation and hygiene in health care facilities: Status in low- and middle-income countries and way forward.* Retrieved from WHO website:
http://www.who.int/water_sanitation_health/publications/wash-health-care-facilities/en

[20] WHO/UNICEF Joint Monitoring Programme (JMP) for Water Supply and Sanitation. (2010) Progress on Sanitation and Drinking-Water, 2010 Update

[21] World Health Organization and UNICEF Joint Monitoring Programme (JMP). (2014). Progress on Drinking Water and Sanitation, 2014 Update. And World Health Organization. (2012). Global costs and benefits of drinking-water supply and sanitation interventions to reach the MDG target and universal coverage. And WHO/UNICEF Joint Monitoring Programme (JMP) for Water Supply and Sanitation. (2010). Progress on Sanitation and Drinking-Water, 2010 Update

[22] Guerrant, RL, et al. Early Childhood Diarrhea Predicts Impaired School Performance. *The Pediatric Infectious Disease Journal.* 2006; 25(6): 513-20.

[23] WHO, *Safer Water, Better Health: Costs, Benefits and Sustainability to Interventions to Protect and Promote Health,* 2008.

[24] USAID (2014). *Multi-sectoral Nutrition Strategy 2014-2025.* Retrieved from USAID website:
https://www.usaid.gov/nutrition-strategy

to consume and digest their food so that those calories and nutrients are not wasted by preventable waterborne diarrheal disease. An important new component of food security and nutrition may be preventing waste. This type of collaboration may well lead to better educational outcomes as well, as children would be healthier both physically and mentally. I applaud USAID's Deputy Assistant Administrator and Global Water Coordinator Chris Holmes for his passionate support for this approach.

WASH and Education: I was once asked: *"How do you know if a primary school in Africa has water and sanitation facilities?"* The answer: There are flowers outside the school, and students – girl students in particular – inside the school. "WASH in Schools" is an emerging priority in the WASH sector, with evidence becoming more clear about the extent to which WASH increases both enrollment and retention rates, particularly for girl students. Young girls should be carrying schoolbooks instead of dirty water on their heads, and older girls should have access to both privacy and menstrual hygiene products so that they are able to remain in school during puberty.

Improving WASH conditions in schools can help to prevent worm infestations, of which the vast majority of annual cases globally can be attributed to poor sanitation and hygiene.[25] Studies have shown that the average IQ loss per worm infestation is 3.75 points, representing nearly 633 million IQ points lost among students living in the world's lowest-income countries.[26] Research shows that for every 10 percent increase in female literacy, a country's economy can also grow by 0.3 percent.[27] This is because girls who can stay in school can become better educated and this, in turn, improves their economic output.

There is a great deal of work underway on the "WASH in Schools" front by many stakeholders in the U.S. and far beyond. One example: I would draw the Subcommittees' attention to the support that Coca Cola is providing through its "Support My School" program in India, and in particular to its work to provide boy/girl sanitation facilities and safe drinking water to Kheadaha High School's (near Kolkata) students, over 95% of whom come from poor tribal communities. Indrani Mondal, a student who is the "Prime Minister" of the "Child Cabinet" at the school credits the program with an increase in student enrollment. This is one of the 600 schools that Coca-Cola's "Support My School" has supported to date throughout 22 states in India.

---

[25] Prüss-Üstün, A, et al. (2008). *Safer Water, Better Health: Costs, benefits and sustainability of interventions to protect and promote health.* World Health Organization, Geneva.
[26] WHO. (2005). *Report of the Third Global Meeting of the Partners for Parasite Control: Deworming for health and development.*
[27] Brocklehurst, C. (2004). *The Case for Water and Sanitation: Better water and sanitation make good fiscal and economic sense, and should be prominent in PRSPs and budget allocations.* Sector Finance Working Paper, no. 11. World Bank Water and Sanitation Program. Retrieved from:
http://www.wsp.org/sites/wsp.org/files/publications/af_makingcase.pdf

Menstrual hygiene management is also an important and severely under-recognized part of WASH in Schools efforts. Female students who have reached puberty, as well as female teachers, require a private, clean, and dignified place in which to take care of their personal needs. When schools do not offer such facilities, many girls have reported being unwilling or unable to attend school while menstruating resulting in absenteeism 10-20 percent of the time.[28] Providing private, safe, and improved sanitation facilities for girls at school is one important solution for improving girls' education around the world.

WASH and Democracy: I spent last week in South America with the Avina Foundation meeting with hundreds of community water association leaders from 24 countries across Latin America. After working with and learning from these groups for four years, I would assert that oftentimes the best primary school for democracy is the village water committee. This is particularly true for women who often first experience participatory democracy when they are voting for local leaders on such a committee. The World Justice Project out of Seattle, Washington has also explored the increasingly clear linkages between development and democratization.

Momentum on Capitol Hill and at USAID

My colleagues, partners and I are grateful for the continued and growing congressional support for this issue at the least since the Water for the Poor Act of 2005 and for the continued and growing support from the Bush and Obama Administrations. We are optimistic about the current momentum for WASH on both ends of Pennsylvania Avenue:

1) USAID is nearing the end of the second year of its five-year Water and Development Strategy, launched in 2013 with strong bipartisan support.[29] Under the leadership of former Administrator Shah and Acting Administrator Lenhardt, USAID is making steady progress toward increasing the effectiveness of its programming on global WASH. The vast majority of its work focuses on the linkages between WASH and human health, and the agency is also positioning both water and sanitation as pivotal to meeting other important development challenges: food security and under-nutrition, Neglected Tropical Diseases, primary education, poverty alleviation, and opportunities for girls. My colleagues and I look forward to continuing to work with USAID and the Department of State to further prioritize WASH as an important sector in its own right, and to demonstrate the contributions WASH can continue to make to related programs across U.S. foreign policy.
2) The Water for the World Act was passed without objection late in 2014 and signed into law. This legislation significantly strengthens the Water for the Poor Act of 2005 in part by ensuring that our WASH programming is targeted to help the

[28] Lopez-Quintero, C., Freeman. P., & Neumark, Y. (2009). Hand Washing Among School Children in Bogotá, Colombia. *American Journal of Public Health.* 99(1), 94-101.
[29] http://www.usaid.gov/documents/1865/usaid-water-and-development-strategy-2013-2018

world's poorest, and by increasing the monitoring and evaluation of projects, particularly after the technical phase of the implementation. It also reinforces what I perceive to be the ongoing sense of Congress that the vast majority of these water and sanitation efforts should continue to focus primarily on the linkages between WASH and public health across the developing world.

3) We are seeing more meaningful, more leveraged programming by USAID and its partners, positioning WASH at the forefront of modernizing foreign assistance. Our job in the international donor community is to get out of the aid business by helping to move countries to aid-independence. The examples I have shared above show how, with your support, the WASH sector is driving toward foreign assistance reform principles, including *"accountability through transparency, evaluation and learning; and country ownership of the priorities and resources for, and implementation of, development"* as advocated for by the Modernizing Foreign Assistance Network.[30]

4) We continue to see strong support for global water and sanitation challenges from Americans across the country. Private philanthropists like the Bill and Melinda Gates Foundation, Conrad N. Hilton Foundation, and Skoll Foundation; civic groups like Rotary International; thousands of church groups, primary and high schools; large corporate philanthropies, social entrepreneurs, universities (including the University WASH Network), Americans leading global efforts such as the Global Sanitation Fund, and thousands of nonprofits are making significant contributions.

5) We are also pleased that, even in a difficult budget climate, Congress continues to appropriate the funds necessary to maintain its commitment to the Water for Poor Act of 2005, now as amended by the Water for the World Act of 2014. This year the House Appropriations Committee has maintained level funding, and urged that $135 million of the total be directed to sub-Saharan Africa (recommended). Its Senate counterpart has recommended a funding level of $400m – a welcome increase of $17.5 million – further underscoring the importance that Congress places on safe drinking water and sanitation as a priority of U.S. foreign policy.

6) Most importantly, we see leadership on water and sanitation from developing countries themselves, leading toward self-sufficiency and an eventual end to U.S. and other aid. In the Financing For Development[31] meeting in Ethiopia recently, we saw significantly increased interest in Domestic Resource Mobilization that would increase the amount of public and private resources in developing countries themselves going to development priorities. We are likely to see increasingly strong commitments from countries throughout Africa, Asia, and Latin America to meet the Sustainable Development Goals, including universal coverage of water and sanitation by 2030. Also, the scale and scope of the Sanitation and Water for All Partnership[32] (a global partnership to ensure that all people have access to basic

---

[30] http://www.modernizeaid.net/thewayforward.html
[31] http://www.un.org/esa/ffd/ffd3
[32] http://www.sanitationandwaterforall.org

sanitation and safe drinking water by improving government prioritization and accountability, strengthening in-country planning processes, and enhancing monitoring and evaluation) is increasing, and we are seeing increased budgets and strengthened national policies for WASH across the globe. Those budgets and policies increasingly meet the needs of everyone in their countries – rural, urban, and peri-urban - not just relatively wealthy people on or near the grid. Particularly impressive are the efforts of Indian Prime Minister Narendra Modi. He has announced the Swachh Bharat Abhiyan[33] (Clean India Campaign) through which he aims to achieve universal coverage of sanitation by Mahatma Gandhi's 150th birthday – October 2, 2019 - leading to a much more secure India from a health and economic security standpoint.

Recommendations

To accomplish these WASH and related goals requires a dedicated, focused water team at USAID, and continued strong leadership from Capitol Hill. To support and strengthen these efforts, and knowing of the Chairmen's and the Subcommittees' desire for tangible recommendations, we respectfully request that the U.S. Congress:

- *Continue to provide strong congressional oversight.* From the Water for the Poor Act, signed into law by then-President Bush in 2005, to the Water for the World Act of 2014, through annual appropriations, it appears that the sense of congress remains quite consistent and bipartisan. These laws and the funds appropriated to implement them are very much about improving public health through WASH. For example, the priority of the Water for the World Act is the list of countries in the WASH Needs Index, i.e. those people who suffer most from water- and sanitation-related health challenges. I encourage the Subcommittees to reach out to the Administration more frequently, including an additional hearing. A partial list of questions I would encourage Congress to ask:
  - o As called for by recent legislation and appropriations bills, is the vast majority of this funding going to the countries and communities suffering most from a lack of access (including but not limited to first-time access) to WASH and therefore from high WASH-related disease burdens? A continued focus on people and their health may best position water and sanitation as a means to preventing and mitigating the severity of emerging threats and building economic prosperity.
  - o Is the funding being invested in longterm, viable WASH programs as envisaged by the Water for the Poor Act and the Water for the World Act? Is the Administration continuing in its trajectory to build capacity in developing countries, not just provide services? Have we drilled our last well as an

---

[33] https://en.wikipedia.org/wiki/Swachh_Bharat_Abhiyan

international donor? Are those funds being invested in programs that decentralize project ownership to the most local possible level? Are we investing U.S. taxpayer funds in programs that are viable and appropriate from technical, financial, and socio-cultural standpoints?

o Are those funds being spent in a way that positions WASH as the path toward more effective foreign assistance, including the aims of the Modernizing Foreign Assistance Network - accountability through transparency, evaluation and learning; and country ownership of the priorities and resources for, and implementation of, development?

- *Congress should urge USAID to be a more catalytic stakeholder in water and sanitation*, focused more on outcomes than on inputs. USAID and its partners have an opportunity to focus less on direct service provision, and more on capacity-strengthening. The goal is to leave behind capacity so that the local communities can solve their own problems long after we leave. A key part of this is to support monitoring and evaluation particularly "post project," so that any problems after the technical end of the project are resolved – ideally by local communities - in a longlasting fashion. Effective, appropriate programming like that envisioned in USAID's water strategy leads not only to water and sanitation successes, but to aid independence and stronger trading partners.

- *Increase appropriations for WASH to the greatest extent possible.* WASH is a pivotal, fundamental issue. Success in WASH leads to better outcomes for related development objectives (health, education, gender empowerment, economic development, etc.) A lack of WASH impedes progress across the development spectrum. Specifically for FY16, we ask the House to recede to the Senate-recommended level of $400m for water and sanitation.

- *Please visit a WASH program in the field* – take your families and your colleagues in Congress with you. Become a WASH storyteller. Nothing compares to seeing firsthand the results achieved by U.S. public and private support for WASH.

- *Find a way to provide USAID the authority to hire additional qualified staff* in the Water Office and throughout the agency, in DC and beyond. WASH is both an emerging threat and an emerging opportunity and USAID could build significant additional capacity in this area.

- *Use WASH as an opportunity to strengthen ties between the U.S. and our strongest allies* (e.g. continue to build on the sanitation programs currently underway in India, funded by USAID and the Bill and Melinda Gates Foundation) and between the U.S. and fragile states (e.g. make WASH a more prominent piece of our relationship with governments across the Sahel).

- *Encourage more partnerships* between the U.S. Government and Americans in all 50 states, e.g. Rotary and other civic groups, faith-based organizations, and American schoolchildren.

- *Look for leveraged and innovative finance opportunities* to increase the impact of taxpayer funds. Two examples: 1) efforts are underway to assist Domestic Resource

Mobilization in developing countries, and to make sure those domestic funds (both increased taxpayer revenues and private capital) are used for fundamental development needs including WASH, and 2) USAID's Development Credit Authority, where limited U.S. taxpayer exposure makes available a great deal of local credit.
- *Support and urge the Administration to do even more to support the Sustainable Development Goals* (to be finalized in September 2015) and their likely focus on universal coverage of WASH by 2030.
- *Continue to look for ways to clarify and support legislatively the linkages between WASH and many other development challenges*, including but not limited to the:
    o Global Food Security Act
    o Reach Every Mother and Child Act
    o Neglected Tropical Diseases Act
    o African Health Systems Strengthening Act

A former colleague of yours, Rep. Jim Leach, said a few years ago:

> *"In our interactions with the world the US basically only has two options. We can emphasize our capacities to project military might and be a global policeman or we can emphasize our humanitarian concerns and be a global doctor or engineer...American leadership in the 21st century will be judged on whether the US chooses to be a superhumanitarian power rather than principally a military interventionist... One of the myths of our time is that realism is about might. Actually realism is about the human condition. It is the human condition that must be improved if national security is to be strengthened. Impoverished nations are breeding grounds for radicalism. Where there is no hope there is nothing to lose."*

Your actions on the Hill make a meaningful difference to the lives of millions across Africa, Asia, and Latin America, and comprise a very small piece of the federal budget. The WASH sector is well-placed to work with you to get the biggest bang for our buck from these programs by increasing the effectiveness of U.S. foreign assistance, and contributing to the success of related development sectors – health, girls' education, poverty alleviation, hunger/under-nutrition, and others. I also feel confident that your leadership will catalyze more support from U.S. citizens via their civic groups, faith groups, private and corporate philanthropies, school groups, and academia.

I am grateful for the progress being made, and encourage you to explore ways to do even more, in partnership with the Administration and Americans from across the country. The global water and sanitation challenge is indeed an emerging threat, but more importantly it provides a genuine leadership opportunity for America. This challenge is serious but solvable. It is being solved as we speak, and with your continued leadership we can ensure that the millions of people in the world who lack safe drinking water and sanitation can live their lives with dignity, safety and economic prosperity.

Mr. ROHRABACHER. Mr. Bilodeau.

STATEMENT OF MR. DENIS BILODEAU, 1ST VICE PRESIDENT, ORANGE COUNTY WATER DISTRICT BOARD OF DIRECTORS

Mr. BILODEAU. Thank you, Chairmen Rohrabacher and Smith and members of the subcommittee. I am Denis Bilodeau and I appear before you today as an elected member of the Board of Directors of the Orange County Water District. I am honored to appear before you to discuss global water scarcity. I will summarize my statement and request that it be submitted into the formal hearing record.

As background, the OCWD is located in the 48th Congressional District in Southern California. We provide groundwater to 19 cities and water agencies with a population of 2.4 million. OCWD has led the way in developing innovative water solutions across a range of technology and infrastructure.

In the late 1980s, we recognized that to preserve our region's economic vitality we needed to address groundwater depletion, seawater intrusion, and unreliable surface water supplies. We implemented an aggressive program to develop a water treatment process with our sister agency, which is the Orange County Sanitization District. This is called the Groundwater Replenishment System. This system takes treated wastewater from the Orange County Sanitation District—and when I say treated wastewater, I speak of sewage—that would otherwise be discharged into the Pacific Ocean. It implements a three-step advanced treatment process that consists of microfiltration, reverse osmosis, and ultraviolet light with hydrogen peroxide. This treatment and purification process produces high-quality water that exceeds all State and Federal drinking water standards and delivers enough water to serve 850,000 people with the production of 100 million gallons a day currently.

When we think about global water supply needs and the ways in which to reduce tensions that arise from constrained potable water supplies and the ability to share experiences, collaboration is important. OCWD shares its knowledge in advanced water purification technology.

For example, Singapore enhanced its water security using our experience and expertise. The country of Singapore has been principally reliant on water from Malaysia. With political differences between the nations, and the expiration of long-term agreements for water transfers between Malaysia and Singapore, the Public Utility Board of Singapore was tasked with finding ways to make Singapore more water self-sufficient. The Singapore PUB reached out to us to learn about technology that our district was using to purify wastewater and put it back into the groundwater supplies. Water leaders from Singapore visited us to see what we were doing to recycle and purify wastewater and to see how we were communicating with the public to bolster public support for potable reuse.

Working with us, Singapore developed both purified water, which they call NEWater, and seawater desalinization to diversify their portfolio of available water for sources for the drinking water system, as well as to protect against depletion of their reserves during drought or interruption of imported supplies. Singapore also built a secondary system to enable it to serve high purity water to its high-tech customers, such as wafer fabricators and circuit board manufacturers that require highly purified water.

This system of water distribution helped to make Singapore a desirable place for valuable industrial customers and to help locate manufacturing facilities.

In 2014, the Orange County Water District was presented with the Lee Kuan Yew Water Prize for our efforts toward solving the world's water problems by applying innovative technology solutions.

We are proud to serve as a global water leader in the water industry, and at the same time it is just a start. Greater investments must be made to implement similar projects around the world. We must continue to create opportunities for water experts to engage with one another and to exchange information to keep pushing the envelope and develop new and innovative solutions to global water problems.

The Singapore-Orange County Water District collaboration is an example of how American technology transfer can lead to solutions for global water supply and quality needs for regions around the world. Again, the Orange County Water District greatly appreciates the subcommittee's decision to explore this important national and international water security matter. Thank you very much for having me.

[The prepared statement of Mr. Bilodeau follows:]

ORANGE COUNTY WATER DISTRICT
Orange County's Groundwater Authority

TESTIMONY

OF

MR. DENIS BILODEAU

FIRST VICE PRESIDENT
AND
MEMBER
BOARD OF DIRECTORS

ORANGE COUNTY WATER DISTRICT
FOUNTAIN VALLEY, CALIFORNIA

PRESENTED BEFORE

SUBCOMMITTEE ON AFRICA, GLOBAL HEALTH, GLOBAL HUMAN RIGHTS, AND
INTERNATIONAL ORGANIZATIONS
AND
SUBCOMMITTEE ON EUROPE, EURASIA AND EMERGING THREATS

COMMITTEE ON FOREIGN AFFAIRS

U.S. HOUSE OF REPRESENTATIVES

WASHINGTON, D.C. 20515

SEPTEMBER 9, 2015

Mr. Chairman, members of the Subcommittee, I am Denis Bilodeau and I appear before you as an elected member of the board of directors for the Orange County Water District (OCWD). I am deeply honored to appear before the Subcommittee to discuss one of the most pressing issues of our times. OCWD is located in Southern California and provides groundwater to Orange County including the 19 cities and water agency's we serve. They include the cities of Anaheim, Buena Park, Fountain Valley, Fullerton, Garden Grove, Huntington Beach, La Palma, Newport Beach, Tustin, Orange, Santa Ana, Westminster, Seal Beach and the East Orange County Water District, Golden State Water Company, Irvine Ranch Water District, Mesa Water District, Serrano Water District, and Yorba Linda Water District, which serve more than 2.4 million citizens and businesses.

Since 1933, OCWD has taken pride in advancing the development of sustainable water supplies to address a growing population and changes in precipitation patterns. This commitment is demonstrated vividly by our recently expanded Groundwater Replenishment System (GWRS). The GWRS is the world's largest advanced water purification system for potable reuse. It takes treated wastewater that otherwise would be sent to the Pacific Ocean and purifies it using a three-step advanced process.

OCWD is pleased to be part of today's hearing into the national security implications associated with an uncertain water supply future. We all know the statistics that illustrate how scarce our freshwater supplies are becoming. What is also becoming better known is the real consequences to the world's geopolitical order as potable water supplies become less secure. Simply stated, drought, population increases, pollution and other factors impacting water supplies manifest in conflict, starvation and significant shifts in migration by populations seeking a better human condition. All of this creates political and economic challenges for us as a nation. And from a domestic perspective, if we do not have a reliable supply of water, the impacts on food production, industrial production and recreational activities are dramatic with reverberations to our domestic economy.

Today, I would like to address these issues by discussing how OCWD and its partner the Orange County Sanitation District (OCSD) has developed a meaningful response to the drought conditions that we have experienced for almost a decade and the incredible severity of the drought during the past four years. It has often been stated that California has always met challenges and succeeded, defying the conventional wisdom that our state is too big and the problems are too big to find a long-lasting solution. In the case of water supply, OCWD and OCSD have taken a big problem, challenging meterological conditions, and designed a solution that delivers long-term water security for our region that can be replicated throughout the arid and semi-arid regions of our nation and the world.

In Orange County, we live in a desert. The base flow of the Santa Ana River, our main source of surface water, continues to decline. Imported water supplies from Northern California and Colorado are restricted. We expect droughts to occur three out of every 10 years. Population growth within our region is expected to increase and so will water demands. There was and is a need.

In the late 1980's OCWD recognized that to preserve our region's economic and social vitality the challenges of our groundwater depletion, seawater intrusion and unreliable surface water supplies demanded an innovative solution. OCWD implemented an aggressive program to develop a novel water treatment process with our sister agency, the Orange County Sanitation District. This initiative grew into the Groundwater Replenishment System (GWRS).

Unlike traditional approaches to water treatment, our approach recognized that wastewater is a valuable resource. The ability to design a technological approach that would capture this resource, remove the impurities and recycle it back into the environment would address multiple needs ranging from supplementing water supply to protecting our natural resources.

The GWRS takes treated wastewater from OCSD that otherwise would be discharged into the Pacific Ocean. It implements a sophisticated process to purify this water. The process involves using a three-step advanced treatment process that consists of microfiltration, reverse osmosis, and ultraviolent light with hydrogen peroxide. This treatment and purification process produces high-quality water that exceeds all state and federal drinking water standards. Let me emphasize this point. OCWD is able to exceed public health standards in developing a sustainable water supply.

GWRS has allowed our region to take control of our future. However, this effort has been achieved in a partnership with federal and state agencies that provided vital assistance in making this project a reality. Today, the partnership is responsible for delivering enough drinking water for 850,000 people with a production of 100 million gallons of water per day.

As much as GWRS is providing an important water supply, GWRS is also important for the message it sends to other water scarce regions of the nation and the world. GWRS is a project based upon a local solution grounded in local control, reliability and a high-quality water supply. The opportunity to implement a proven approach like GWRS can return important dividends to political and economic security needs.

Water reuse occurs in various ways throughout the world. It happens daily on rivers and other water bodies everywhere. If you live in a community downstream of another, chances are you are reusing its water and likewise communities downstream of you are most likely reusing your water.

There is no one-size-fits-all solution to water reuse. GWRS establishes a technology foundation to design and build individual approaches to sustainable water supply needs. Water needs of a specific community, water sources, public health regulations, costs, and the types of water infrastructure in place, such as distribution systems, man-made reservoirs or natural groundwater basins, determine if and how your reused water becomes part of the drinking water supply.

As the state of California faces severe drought conditions, increased attention is turned to local projects like the GWRS that provide reliable water supplies.

When we think about global water supply needs and ways in which to reduce tensions that arise from constrained potable water supplies, the ability to share experiences and promote collaboration is important. OCWD shares its knowledge in advanced water purification technology. It helped Singapore to enhance its own national water security. Today, Singapore is considered a shining example of how a nation state can effectively meet its water scarcity challenges.

Singapore learned the lesson of water supply vulnerability in the early days of WWII, when the Japanese cut off the water supply from Malaysia on which the Island of Singapore was dependent, leading to the rapid surrender of British forces.

Even in recent years, the country of Singapore has been principally reliant on water from Malaysia. With political differences between the nations and the expiration of long-term agreements for water transfers between Malaysia and Singapore, the Public Utilities Board of Singapore (PUB) was tasked with finding ways to make Singapore more water self-sufficient.

The Singapore PUB reached out to OCWD to learn about the technology that the District used to purify wastewater back into the groundwater supplies. Water leaders from Singapore visited OCWD to see what we were doing to recycle and purify wastewater and how we were communicating with the public to bolster public support for potable reuse.

Working with the information gained from OCWD's successes, Singapore developed both purified water, which they call NEWater, and seawater desalination to diversify their portfolio of available water sources for the drinking water system and to protect against depletion of their reserves during periods of drought or interruption of imported supplies.

Singapore also recognized the critical role this water supply provides to its industrial economic engine. It built a secondary water distribution system to enable it to serve high-purity water to high-technology customers, such as wafer fabricators and circuit board manufacturers, who need higher purified water for their manufacturing processes. This system of high-purity recycled water distribution helped to make Singapore a desirable place for valuable industrial customers to locate manufacturing facilities. Most of the NEWater produced in Singapore is used by industrial customers.

The contributions that OCWD has made to advancing the technological capabilities of developing safe and sustainable water supplies was recognized at the 2014 Singapore International Water Week. The Lee Kuan Yew Water Prize was presented to the Orange County Water District. This distinguished prize honors outstanding contributions by individuals or organizations toward solving the world's water problems by applying innovative technologies or implementing policies and programs that benefit humanity.

This prize is a tremendous achievement for OCWD and we are proud to serve as a global leader in the water industry. However, at the same time, it is just the start. Greater investments must be made to implement similar projects around the world. We must continue to create opportunities for water experts to engage with one another and exchange information to keep pushing the envelope and develop new and innovative solutions to global water problems.

The Singapore/Orange County Water District's example is that of a technology transfer and collaboration to solve global water supply and quality problems. This kind of collaboration delivers tangible benefits in the form of improved quality of life, robust economic activity, public health improvements, and long-term socio-economic stability. The lessons that OCWD has learned in its decades of developing and implementing responses to water scarcity demands a meaningful partnership among various local, regional, state national and international agencies to ensure the development of sustainable water supplies that, in turn, will reduced, if not eliminate, the potential for conflict related to unreliable water supplies.

Again, OCWD deeply appreciates the subcommittee's decision to explore this important national and international security matter. I would be happy to respond to any questions the subcommittee might have.

Mr. ROHRABACHER. Mr. Whittington.

STATEMENT OF DALE WHITTINGTON, PH.D., PROFESSOR, UNIVERSITY OF NORTH CAROLINA

Mr. WHITTINGTON. Mr. Chairman, just by chance, I just got back from 7 weeks in Singapore and had the privilege of seeing these facilities that Denis has just described. So everything he is saying is true here. I just was at the Lee Kuan Yew School.

Thank you very much for the invitation to speak today on the role of improved water and sanitation services and avoiding conflict and building economic prosperity. I would like to make three points in my testimony.

First, there is good news from the public health field. Thanks in part to the efforts of the United States and the international community, childhood mortality rates are declining in developing countries and the rate of decline is accelerating. And as we look ahead over the next few decades, economic growth should enable East Asia, Southeast Asia, Latin America to solve their water supply and sanitation problems and thankfully water-related mortality will be a thing of the past in these regions. The remaining challenges are going be to be in South Asia and Sub-Saharan Africa, but even here childhood diarrhea and mortality rates are falling rapidly.

However, the economic benefits from investments in water and sanitation infrastructure consist of both health and nonhealth outcomes, and Denis has just described some of the nonhealth outcomes in Singapore. There is a shift occurring in the relative magnitude of these two components with the health benefits declining and the nonhealth benefits, such as time savings, increasing.

The nonhealth related benefits of improved water services vary depending on location, but they can be surprisingly large and are often increasing. For example, in a recent study conducted in Kathmandu, Nepal, researchers at the Institute of Water Policy at the National University of Singapore found that from 2001 to 2014 the real cost after adjusting for inflation that households were incurring coping with water shortages and intermittent contaminated supplies actually doubled from $7 a month to $14 a month on average. These coping costs include the value of time spent collecting water from outside the home, investments in water storage, in-house water treatment, and expenditures to water vendors, all of which most Americans never experience.

Investments in improved water services that reduce or eliminate these coping costs free up a household's time, just as John just mentioned, and money for other priorities and increase economic growth. It is really hard for an urban economy to function efficiently if everyone is worried about getting home from work to meet a tanker truck in order to have sufficient water for a week.

I think that this shift from health to nonhealth benefits has important implications for donor assistance in the WASH sector. In places where coping costs are high, one can be confident that the economic benefits of improved water supplies will also be very high. But the coping costs are not high everywhere, and careful economic analysis of water and sanitation infrastructure projects is needed to ensure that assistance is targeted to communities where it will have the greatest economic impact. This will also go a large way to reducing conflict. The best way to avoid conflict is for a country to get on a high-growth development path.

My second point is that the world's population is becoming increasingly urbanized and the largest economic benefits of improved water and sanitation infrastructure usually will be in cities in developing countries. So if the objective is to promote economic growth, then it is important to prioritize investments in urban areas.

Large economic benefits can be obtained not only from infrastructure investment, but also from policy reforms. Utilities in cities in low- and middle-income countries almost always provide water and sanitation services to customers far below cost. They rely on subsidies from higher-level governments and donors to pay these subsidies. And recent research has shown that these subsidies are very poorly targeted. The majority don't reach poor households.

For my third point I want to shift from the economic benefits of water and sanitation investments to the relationship between water and conflict on international rivers. I know this subcommittee has heard from Paul Sullivan and his testimony on the implications of the Grand Renaissance Dam in Ethiopia. However, I have been studying and writing about the Nile for almost 40 years, and I would be happy to answer any further questions you have about the situation that is emerging on the Nile. I would like to just say a few last things and comments on that situation.

The construction of the Grand Ethiopian Renaissance Dam started in 2011 on the Blue Nile near the Ethiopian-Sudanese border. It is now about 40 percent complete. When it is finished the Nile riparians and the global community will face a new situation in transboundary hydropolitics. There will be two very large dams, the Aswan High Dam and the GERD, with over-year storage capacity on the same river in different countries in a water-scarce basin, and there is presently no plan for coordinating the operation of those large storage facilities.

In my judgment, the Nile riparians need assistance from the international community immediately in reaching a fair, equitable agreement on the joint operation of the Aswan High Dam and the GERD based on best global practices. This is a matter of urgency. Ethiopia will likely begin filling the GERD in 2016, just next year.

So in summary, I have four recommendations. First, in order to promote economic growth, assistance in the water supply and sanitation sector should be focused on South Asia and Sub-Saharan African cities.

Second, if USAID wants water and sanitation investments with high economic returns, it should assist countries to do the economic analysis to identify where economic returns will be greatest. President Reagan's Executive Order 12291 required that all major regulations in the United States pass a cost-benefit test. Why not have USAID assistance to the water sector pass a similar test?

Third, the United States Agency for International Development's global water coordinator and the Department of State's special advisor for water resources should give high priority to the reform of municipal water pricing and tariffs in developing countries and to improve the targeting of available subsidies to poor households.

And finally, fourth, the United States Department of State should encourage international organizations such as the World Bank to reengage in the Nile mission. As I said, this is a matter of urgency for the international community.

Thank you very much.

[The prepared statement of Mr. Whittington follows:]

THE UNIVERSITY
of NORTH CAROLINA
at CHAPEL HILL

DEPARTMENT OF ENVIRONMENTAL
SCIENCES AND ENGINEERING

166 ROSENAU HALL   T 919.966.1171
CAMPUS BOX 7431   F 919.966.7911
CHAPEL HILL, NC 27599-7431
www.sph.unc.edu/envr

Written Testimony by

Prof. Dale Whittington[1]

Departments of Environmental Sciences & Engineering, and
City & Regional Planning

University of North Carolina at Chapel Hill

Wednesday, September 9, 2015

House Committee on Foreign Affairs

Joint Subcommittee Hearing:
The Role of Water in Avoiding Conflict and Building Prosperity

---

[1] Email: Dale_Whittington@unc.edu

Thank you for the invitation to speak today on the role of improved water and sanitation services in avoiding conflict and building economic prosperity. I would like to make three points.

First, there is good news from the public health field: in developing countries childhood mortality rates are declining & the rate of decline is accelerating (Rajaratnam et al. 2010, Lozano et al., 2011). As we look ahead over the next few decades, it is likely that economic growth will enable East Asia, Southeast Asia, and Latin America to solve their water supply and sanitation problems, and WASH-related mortality will be a thing of the past in these regions (Jeuland et al., 2013). The remaining challenges will be in South Asia and Sub-Saharan Africa, but even here childhood diarrhea and mortality rates are falling rapidly.

However, the economics benefits of investments in water and sanitation infrastructure consist of both health and nonhealth outcomes. There is a shift occurring in the relative magnitude of these two components, with the health benefits declining and the nonhealth benefits—especially time savings and other quality-of-life improvements—increasing.

The nonhealth-related benefits of improved water services vary depending on local conditions, but can be surprisingly large. A recent study of households living in communities outside of Meru, Kenya, found that the total costs associated with coping with poor quality, unreliable water supplies were approximately US$20 per month on average, almost 5% of reported monthly cash income (Cook et al., 2015). These coping costs include the value of time spent collecting water from outside the home, investments in water storage and in-house treatment, and expenditures to water vendors. Coping costs were greater than 10% of income for one-quarter of the households in the study. They were also higher among poorer households. These coping costs are higher than average household water bills in some communities in the United States and much higher than average household water bills in Nairobi. Investments in improved water services that reduce or eliminate these coping costs free up a household's time and money for other priorities, and may increase economic growth.

As another example, in a recent study conducted in Kathmandu, Nepal, researchers at the Institute of Water Policy at the Lee Kuan Yew School of Public Policy, National University of Singapore, found that from 2001 to 2014, the costs households were incurring coping with water shortages and intermittent, contaminated supplies doubled in real terms from about US$7 per month to US$14 per month (Gurung et al. 2015). Even incurring coping costs of US$14 per month did not alleviate all of stress and discomfort that a household experienced trying to obtain water from contaminated wells, tanker truck vendors, and piped connections that supply water only a few hours a week. It is hard for an urban economy to function efficiently if people are worried about getting home from work to meet a tanker truck in order to have sufficient water for a week.

This shift from health to nonhealth benefits has important implications for donor assistance in the WASH sector. In places where coping costs are high, one can be confident that the economic benefits of improved water supplies also will be very high. But the coping costs will not be high everywhere, and careful economic analysis of water and sanitation infrastructure projects is needed to ensure that assistance is targeted to communities where it will have the greatest economic impact.

This call for greater economic analysis of water and sanitaiton investments will be controversial because it is hard to quantify all of the benefits of WASH projects. This is in part because the causal links between water-related investments and economic growth run in both directions. Water-related investments can increase economic productivity and growth, and economic growth provides the resources to finance capital-intensive investments in water-related infrastructure. Moreover, water-related investments result in two conceptually different types of economic benefits. They can reduce the losses experienced from water-related hazards and at the same time produce valued goods and services (Sadoff et al. 2015). Water-related investments also increase human well-being without increasing national income or economic growth as conventionally measured.

The relationship between water and economic growth varies with the local context. As in other sectors of the economy, there are investments with both high and low economic returns. Although the economic analysis is difficult, it is urgently needed because piped network infrastructure is very capital intensive and poor investment decisions are costly. The challenge is to determine the timing and sequencing of investments in a particular location that will yield the highest economic returns. Assistance needs to include building local institutions and analytical capacity to find these economically attractive water and sanitation investments. A simple focus on WASH technology, such as drilling more wells and building more toilets, will not maximize economic benefits.

My second point is that as the world's population becomes increasingly urbanized, the largest economic benefits of improved water and sanitation infrastructure usually will be in cities in developing countries. If the objective is to promote economic growth, then it is important to prioritize water supply and sanitation investments in these cities—especially in poor neighborhoods with the worst services. It is there that the nonhealth economic benefits are likely to be greatest because time savings can be most easily converted into productive labor and increased income.

Large economic benefits can be obtained not only from infrastructure investment, but also from policy reforms. Utilities in cities low and middle-income countries almost always provide piped water and sanitation services to customers far below cost. Utilities have no financial resources to expand and improve services, or to adapt to climate change. They rely on subsidies from higher levels of government and donors to pay for their operations. Recent research has shown that these subsidies are very poorly targeted, and the majority does not reach poor households (Whittington et al. 2015; Fuente et al., 2015).

Not only do current tariff structures fail to target subsidies effectively to poor households, but also they fail to send the correct price signal about the economic value of water, resulting in inefficient water use and poor capacity expansion decisions.

Assistance that helps build local institutions and analytical capacity can enable utilities to both adopt improved tariff structures and design mechanisms to better target available subsidies to poor households.

For my third point I will shift from the economic benefits of water supply and sanitation investments to the relationship between water and conflict on international rivers. I want to focus on the evolving situation on the Nile.

Construction of the Grand Ethiopian Renaissance Dam (GERD) started in 2011, and is now about 40% complete. This dam is located on the Blue Nile in Ethiopia near the Ethiopian-Sudanese border. When it is finished, the Nile riparians and the global community will face a new situation in transboundary hydro-politics. A recent report from the Massachusetts Institute of Technology (2014) describes the challenges this new dam poses for Egypt, Sudan, and Ethiopia. There will be two very large dams (the Aswan High Dam and the GERD) with over-year storage capacity on the same river in different countries in a water-scarce basin.

Presently there is no plan for coordinating the operation of these two large storage facilities. Egypt, Sudan, and Ethiopia signed a "Declaration of Principles" in Khartoum this past March, and this was an important step toward cooperation on the Nile. But there has been little concrete progress made on an agreement for filling the GERD and for the coordinated operation of the GERD and the Aswan High Dam. The countries have even failed to reach agreement on the team of technical consultants to be engaged to help them with this task.

This evolving situation on the Nile deserves the international community's full attention. The United States should do whatever it can to assist the Nile riparians in reaching a fair, equitable agreement on joint operation of the Aswan High Dam and the GERD based on best global practices and experience. This is a matter of considerable urgency. Ethiopia will likely begin filling the GERD in 2016. Without a well-developed, carefully designed joint operating agreement, there is an increasing risk of conflict due to misunderstanding and ambiguity surrounding the different riparians' motives and actions (Whittington et al, 2014).

In summary, I have four recommendations.

First, in order to promote economic growth, the United States Agency for International Development's (USAID) assistance in the water supply and sanitation sector should be largely focused on South Asia and Sub-Saharan Africa, and on cities.

Second, if USAID wants water and sanitation investments with high economic returns, it must assist countries and cities do the economic analysis necessary to identify where the economic returns will be greatest. Assistance with building local institutions and analytical capacity is needed to improve this investment planning process.

Third, USAID's Global Water Coordinator and the Department of State Special Advisor for Water Resources should give high priority to the reform of municipal water pricing and tariffs to improve the targeting of available subsidies to poor households and to promote economic growth.

Fourth, the United States Department of State should increase its diplomatic efforts in the Nile basin and encourage international organizations such as the World Bank to seriously reengage in the Nile. The lack of an agreement on the coordinated operation of the Aswan High Dam and the Grand Ethiopian Renaissance Dam creates unacceptable risks of future conflict.

Thank you.

References

Cook, Joseph, Peter Kimuyi, and Dale Whittington. (2015). "The Costs of Coping with Poor Water Supply in Rural Kenya." EfD Discussion Paper Series EfD DP-15-09. Gothenburg, Sweden.

Fuente, David, Josephine Gakii Gatua, Moses Ikiara, Jane Kabubo-Mariara and Dale Whittington. 2015. "Water and Sanitation Service Delivery, Pricing, and the Poor: An Empirical Estimate of Subsidy Incidence in Nairobi, Kenya." EfD Discussion Paper Series 15-17.

Gurung, Yogendra, Jane Zhao, Bal Kumar KC, Wu Xun, Bhim Suwal, and Dale Whittington. (2015). "The Costs of Delay: A Comparison of 2001 and 2014 Household Water Supply Coping Costs in the Kathmandu Valley, Nepal." Working Paper, Institute of Water Policy, Lee Kuan Yew School of Public Policy. National University of Singapore.

Jeuland, Marc, David Fuente, Semra Ozdemir, Maura Allaire, and Dale Whittington. (2013). "The long-term dynamics of morality benefits from improved water and sanitation in less developed countries." *PLOSone*. October, Vol. 8 Issue 10, p1-16. 16p. DOI: 10.1371/journal.pone.0074804.

Lozano, Rafael; Wang, Haidong; Foreman, Kyle J; Rajaratnam, Julie Knoll; Naghavi, Mohsen; et al. (2011). Progress towards Millennium Development Goals 4 and 5 on maternal and child mortality: an updated systematic analysis. *The Lancet*. Sep 24-Sep 30: 1139-65.

Massachusetts Institute of Technology Non-partisan Eastern Nile Working Group. (2014) *The Grand Ethiopian Renaissance Dam: An Opportunity for Collaboration and Shared Benefits in the Eastern Nile Basin* - An Amicus Brief to the Riparian Nations of Ethiopia, Sudan and Egypt From the International, Convened at the Massachusetts Institute of Technology on 13-14 November 2014, by the MIT Jameel World Water and Food Security Lab.

Rajaratnam, Julie Knoll; Marcus, Jake R; Levin-Rector, Alison; Chalupka, Andrew N; Wang, Haidong; et al. (2010). "Worldwide mortality in men and women aged 15-59 years from 1970 to 2010: a systematic analysis." *The Lancet*. May 15-May 21, 2010: 1704-1720.

Sadoff, Claudia W., James W. Hall, David Grey, J.C.J.H Aerts, Mohamed Ait-Kadi, Casey Brown, Anthony Cox, Simon Dadson, Dustin Garrick, Jerson Kelman, Peter McCornick, Claudia Ringler, Mark Rosegrant, Dale Whittington, and David Wiberg. (2015). *Securing Water, Sustaining Growth: Report of the GWP/OECD Task Force on Water Security and Sustainable Growth*, University of Oxford, UK, 180 pages.

Whittington, Dale, John Waterbury, and Marc Jeuland. (2014). "The Grand Renaissance Dam and Prospects for Cooperation on the Eastern Nile." *Water Policy*. 16: 595–608.

Whittington, Dale, Celine Nauges, David Fuente, Xun Wu. (2015). "A diagnostic tool for estimating the incidence of subsidies delivered by water utilities in low- and medium-income countries, with illustrative simulations." *Utility Policy*. Vol. 34, pp. 70-81.

42

Mr. ROHRABACHER. Thank you very much.

We have been joined by Dan Donovan.

Do you have any opening statement that you would like to make before we go into some questions?

Mr. DONOVAN. No, Mr. Chairman. Thank you very much.

Mr. ROHRABACHER. All right, thank you.

Just I will proceed with my time period here. First of all, about Orange County, I bring people in from all over the world. I must have in the last 10 years brought in 20 or 30 different groups of people from foreign countries to see the operation that is going down there. And it is based on, yes, two elements. One is a new technology with this membrane technology being developed to the utmost, but also it deals with the cooperation of various levels of government. And as you say, the sanitation department and the water district, I don't know if sanitation and water districts get along in other places, but from what I understand, sometimes it is hard for one department of government to talk to the other department of government, whether it is Federal, State, or local.

But just as they are doing that, we need to make sure that at the Federal level we are cooperating between the various departments and agencies that can have an impact on this issue.

And I have already drawn attention to the fact that when you have so many people who are facing a future of billions people without—or a billion people—without clean water, that is a volatile situation where people are seeing their families die, and thus undermine the security and the tranquillity of whatever area that is going on in. For all we know, and I haven't looked at it yet, but I would hope to find out about it, that some of these refugees that are pouring into Europe right now and creating an enormous chaos that Europe just has not been used to, I would say that there probably is a water connection there, and several witnesses have alluded to that.

So when our European friends talk about what can be done to help prevent that, number one, let's make sure people aren't watching their children die of some disease that wouldn't be there if they had clean water, and thus they don't feel compelled about taking their entire family and going to Europe where they think they can get clean water.

Let me ask this. Has there been an assessment? We were talking about trying to have some kind of real assessment as to how effective a program is. Is this lacking? Maybe you could go into a little more detail on that.

Mr. WHITTINGTON. It is hard to do economic analysis of water projects because it is difficult to measure all of these benefits. At the same time, I think we have to try. I mean, the World Bank does it. The Inter-American Development Bank does it. And I think USAID can do it too.

Warren Buffett doesn't get high returns on capital just by chance. I mean, he does the economic analysis to figure that out. And I think it is the same in the water sector. I mean, there are lots of good investments everywhere, but we should be focusing our taxpayer dollars on those investments with the highest economic returns, and you have to do the economic analysis to figure that out.

Mr. ROHRABACHER. And one question for the panel just very quickly. We had the example of Singapore, where you have this huge number of people with a very limited amount of water, and now it is clean water and they are prospering. Is this an urban challenge or are we talking about more of a development challenge in terms of clean water? Just go down the row there.

Mr. OLDFIELD. Sure. Thank you, Mr. Chairman. It is a fair question. We have read the demographic data, 51 percent of the world now lives in cities and urban and peri-urban or informal settlement environments. So I would certainly second Dr. Whittington's suggestion to focus on cities to a certain extent.

But the data also shows that 70 to 75 percent of the remaining problem, 70 to 75 percent of the 663 million people without access to safe drinking water, the 2.4 billion people without a private, safe place to go to the bathroom, are in rural communities.

Mr. ROHRABACHER. Could you please repeat that statistic that you just gave us?

Mr. OLDFIELD. Seventy to seventy-five percent of the remaining need for safe drinking water and sanitation across the developing world is in rural communities, across Africa, across Asia, and across Latin America.

Now, that is changing. People are migrating to cities and informal settlements around cities and so on. So the need is pervasive everywhere.

I think what ties this all together is what I think the three of you said in your opening statements: We know how to solve this. And regardless if it is urban, peri-urban, or rural villages, in Africa, Asia, or Latin America, we know how to solve these problems, they now how to solve these problems, and they need to be solved in a fashion that is both appropriate in technical terms, in financial terms, and in sociocultural terms, and these problems need to be solved in a fashion that is resilient, that is going to build systems that are able to withstand population shifts, droughts, floods, and so on.

So the systems, whether it is urban, peri-urban, or rural, need to be both appropriate in a number of terms, a number of facets of appropriate and resilient.

Mr. BILODEAU. In terms of the Orange County experience, the technology we are using is primarily applicable to urbanized areas because you need to have a central collection point for the wastewater. Then you can then harvest and reuse that water and deliver it back out to your customers. So it wouldn't be so applicable in sparsely populated areas, but definitely for urbanized areas. And our type of system would go hand in hand in terms of development of a sewage collection system, as well as a recycling system along with that.

Mr. ROHRABACHER. So what you have got is sanitation and clean water, again——

Mr. BILODEAU. Combined.

Mr. ROHRABACHER [continuing]. The importance of putting those two together.

Mr. BILODEAU. Yes, developing those in conjunction.

Mr. WHITTINGTON. So I agree with John that there are huge problems in rural areas, but I think that there is a tension between humanitarian aid and pro-growth economic aid. I am not arguing to do less in rural areas. I just want to focus also on urban areas because that is where the economic benefits and the real chance to move economies to a high growth dynamic trajectory is.

And so as people move from rural areas into cities, there is a package of infrastructure investments that are critical to getting economic growth moving, and they include telecommunications and roads and health and education.

And water is a critical component. Piped water services in urban areas are what people want. People in developing countries are just like you. They want 24/7 water that is potable, that they can drink. And this is feasible. And it is not only feasible from a humanitarian point of view, it is the right thing to do from an economic development perspective.

Mr. ROHRABACHER. And of course the cleaner water in the urban area, the less money has to be spent for taking care of people's health problem, and investment in the water would negate some of that cost.

Mr. Smith.

Mr. SMITH. Thank you very much, Mr. Chairman.

Thank you, all three, for your very, very expert and informative presentations.

Let me just ask, Dr. Whittington, you have made four recommendations. Thank you for those. I think they are right on the money and in terms of things we should be doing.

When you talk about the GERD and the Aswan High Dam and the status of the negotiations, my question is, what might a prudent agreement look like? I mean, the time seems to be, you know, coming and quickly passing. I mean, as you pointed out, filling of the dam might begin as early as 2016.

You talk about the U.S. Department of State should increase its diplomatic efforts. What is it doing? How engaged are we? How would you rate it? Is it enough? Is it something we should invite State and USAID to be here to give us some insights and then we could prod them along to try to make this much more serious?

The GAO study has said USAID WASH interventions don't cover large water issues such as dams, as you know. So if you could just give some information or some guidance along those lines.

With regards to sanitation, perhaps one of you, Mr. Oldfield, perhaps you, might want to provide insights and recommendations as to why the international community has failed to meet the MDG targets for sanitation. And even meeting those targets for the accessibility to clean and safe water, yeah, we are talking about having the number of those who don't have access, and that still leaves us, as you know, with over 663 million people who have lacked access to safe water. So it is a step in the right direction, but it is certainly not the achievement of the hope is, which would be universal access. But why is sanitation a laggard?

And let me also ask, in Africa, if it accelerates, as it is, its march to electrification, the Power Africa and other initiatives, how should these emerging economies integrate best practices? And perhaps our friend from Orange County might speak to that.

As you mentioned Mr. Chairman, you have invited delegations from other countries to go and witness what they are doing to share that best practice.

But, I mean, is our government integrating the experts in the field like yourself so that, you know, Nigeria, Ethiopia, name the country, you know, can say: Why reinvent the wheel? This has been perfected to the point, and now that we have access to electricity that we hadn't had before, that state-of-the-art sanitation can be deployed in a way that provides for safety and efficacy of the whole operation.

So if you could speak to that because it seems to me we have written the book on this. We have done this on a whole lot of other issues. We have learned from others, but we also as a country, and I think Europe can say the same thing, has much to share. But if we are not actively integrating that sharing process—you are—but, you know, can it be accelerated, should it be accelerated, and if you could speak to that.

Mr. BILODEAU. Okay, I will go first.

In terms of our experience, we are fortunate that we have very highly qualified engineering companies, private companies, that actually designed and built our facilities for us. The companies are multinational, so they, of course, can go to Singapore, or there is another plant similar to Singapore's in Kuwait that General Electric actually built there and operates it currently.

So in terms of exporting the technology, it is really the American corporations that are leading the way and that have the engineering skill and know-how in terms of the design and the construction.

In terms of at our facility, one thing that we have lended our expertise to is we do a lot of pilot testing of new technologies. There is a new technology called graphene that is in research and development right now that may revolutionize reverse osmosis membranes and bring the cost of reverse osmosis treatment down substantially. And so that is something we are working with Lockheed currently in bench testing basically, their innovation and trying to bring the cost of treating this water down, which, of course, will help to export this technology around the world, and for other applications around the world.

Mr. SMITH. Thank you.

Mr. Oldfield.

Mr. OLDFIELD. Great. Thank you for that question, Mr. Chairman, about sanitation and the MDGs.

There is no easy answer to why the world missed by such a significant amount the Millennium Development Goal for sanitation. I will try in about 10 seconds here. Lack of political will, not just in this country, certainly not just in this country, but more importantly in developing countries, in Africa, Asia, and Latin America, simply a lack of political prioritization, and a lack of financial resources primarily from developing countries for sanitation.

And then in some places where these things did come together, I would use India as an example that made a significant commitment to sanitation throughout 2000 to 2015, there was an imbalance between hardware and software. They built a whole lot of toilets and didn't do the behavior change. They built a lot of hardware and didn't have a lot of software to back that up. So all of a sudden not just in India, but in many other parts of the world you have toilets used for unintended purposes.

If I might take 10 seconds to address the flip side of that, which is how we are going to address the Sustainable Development Goals commitment to universal coverage of sanitation by 2030. It is exactly the opposite. Increased political commitment and prioritization for sanitation, appropriate sanitation solutions, so that all 7-plus billion of us have a place to go to the bathroom on the planet. Political leaders—and I don't mean sanitation ministers or water ministers, I mean prime ministers, finance ministers, heads of state, and heads of government—need to prioritize this, and that is something that we are trying to work on an a bit. And therefore, increased financial support for sanitation primarily from developing countries themselves.

There are a lot of efforts within USAID and up on Capitol Hill to figure out how to best address this concept of domestic resource mobilization, DRM. How can we help mobilize more public and private resources for development challenges, including sanitation, not from this country, not from the international donor community, but from developing countries themselves?

So more political will, more particularly public sector finance. I think we need to redress this imbalance around the world between hardware and software. We need to focus on changing behavior, on changing minds, then the hardware problems will solve themselves, I think. If everybody wants a toilet, the public or the private sector is going to come up with a way to make sure that every single one of those people has a toilet.

And then lastly, echoing your concerns, I haven't seen anything about this GAO audit yet, but from what you have shared with us very briefly, I think I would agree with their concerns. What I would like to see, not just in the sanitation space but in the entire WASH space, is Modernizing Foreign Assistance Network principles of foreign assistance reform, increased accountability, increased capacity, decentralized ownership, and increased transparency throughout our foreign assistance.

Mr. SMITH. On that point, do you believe the political will is emerging, is there, perhaps, to have universal access to adequate sanitation by 2030, facilitated in the post-2015 goals?

Mr. OLDFIELD. I do, whether you mean in the developed world or in the developing world. I mean, this hearing is a manifestation of increased political will for sanitation in developing countries from the United States as one member of the international donor community. The Dutch Government is doing a fantastic job with this, the British Government, the German Government. We have a lot of allies in our renewed focus on sanitation.

But, again, more importantly than that, we are seeing a lot of increased efforts to prioritize sanitation in developing countries. And the one example I would give you is Prime Minister Narenda Modi's commitment to Swachh Bharat Abhiyan, the Clean India campaign.

A year ago, he committed to universal coverage of sanitation in India by October 2, 2019, Mahatma Gandhi's 150th birthday. He is committed to ending open defecation and providing a toilet and making sure it is used for its intended purpose to all of India's 1.25

billion citizens within a very, very short period of time, one example of heightened political will.

Mr. SMITH. Thank you.

Doctor.

Mr. WHITTINGTON. So I will go back to your questions about the Nile, and I think there were two: What would an agreement look like and what is the State Department doing? They are both great questions.

What would an agreement look like? If you go to the Murray-Darling in Australia or you go to the Colorado where you have large over-year storage facilities on big rivers in water-scarce areas, those agreements are hundreds of pages long. And so the first thing is this is not an easy task. I mean, somebody has to actually write these agreements and negotiate these agreements and that takes time and it needs to start very quickly.

Technically, what has to happen in the agreement is that Ethiopia is going to be filling the GERD Reservoir, but they have got to pass enough water down to Sudan and Egypt during that time so that those countries can meet their essential needs. Egypt has the Aswan High Dam, so they can buffer this a little bit if they have storage in the High Dam. Sudan does not. There is no over-year storage in Sudan. So there has to be enough water passed to meet the essential needs of Egypt and Sudan during the filling.

But more importantly, in the long run, there needs to be coordinated management on the droughts, because that is where the real conflict could come, if Ethiopia wants to hold back water on the droughts, and that water is really needed downstream in Sudan and Egypt.

So this is not hard to do technically, but it has to be negotiated. And so the key point on the agreement that we are missing right now, we don't have an agreement, but we also need a trustworthy, binding arbitrator, and that is where I think the global community can come in.

I would say that the State Department is active. They are in Salzburg. The special advisor on water has been working hard. But I think the visibility of this issue really needs to rise. There has not been a coordinated international response on this. It is not just a U.S. concern. It is a concern for Europe and the World Bank. The World Bank has moved back from the Nile, they are not as engaged as they were in the past, and I think this has to change.

Mr. SMITH. Thank you. Thank you.

Mr. ROHRABACHER. Just one thought before we go to Mr. Blumenauer. Cairo, Egypt, do we know how many times it reuses its water? I don't. In many of these countries that we are talking about, they don't reuse it at all. They just use it once and it goes into the ocean. In Orange County, California, how many times do we reuse our water and clean it and reuse it and clean it and reuse it before it goes back into the ocean?

Mr. BILODEAU. Well, now it is infinite. It is dozens of times we continually reprocess the water that comes to us.

Mr. ROHRABACHER. So at least 9, 10 times we are reusing that water. We are purifying it again and then reusing it. And in countries like Egypt on the edge of a desert, this could mean everything, and especially if you end up with a war or something between someone upstream and downstream as compared to just making sure the water you are using, you reuse it over and over again.

Mr. Blumenauer.

Mr. BLUMENAUER. Thank you. And, again, I appreciate the courtesy in permitting me to join the panel.

Dr. Whittington, you mentioned coping costs and cited a study in Nepal, Kathmandu, where they have doubled to being $14 per——

Mr. WHITTINGTON. Per household per month.

Mr. BLUMENAUER. Per household per month, in a nation with a per capita income per household——

Mr. WHITTINGTON. Yes, you have got me there, I think——

Mr. BLUMENAUER. Six hundred dollars, $800?

Mr. WHITTINGTON. Yeah, it is around $1,000, I think. I would have to check, you know. It is a good question. I mean, these may not seem like big numbers to you, but for poor people in developing countries these are high costs. And when households save this money, and as John said, save the time, these can be put to more productive uses and start a country on a path to, you know, economic growth.

But it is really hard to do that if you are spending all of your time, you know, scrambling around a big city trying to figure out how to get water for your family.

Mr. BLUMENAUER. But it struck me, that seems like a very high number to me, thinking about what happens in these developing countries. And it raises the point, I think we are looking at, the number I have heard quoted, 155 million hours a day is spent by women and girls, often, as Mr. Oldfield points out, putting themselves at risk, to secure water for the families, often dirty water. They end up in many developing countries paying a huge amount of their disposable income, to say nothing of money that is not being spent.

I am wondering if you, Doctor, or actually any of the members of the panel would care to comment on our capacity to actually self-fund much of what needs to be done if we are able to get an early intervention, maybe help a little bit of capital expenditure, help a little bit with the planning and development, and as our chairman says, where there are some pretty fundamental areas of savings that aren't being employed. You want to talk about the potential of self-funding this?

Mr. WHITTINGTON. It is a great question, and actually Water.org is doing just this right now with microfinancing water projects in developing countries. So they are putting money into communities that are borrowing and then repaying those loans to get sustainable high-quality water and sanitation services. So I think your point is exactly right. Where coping costs are high, and those savings are real, you know, in dollars and time, there are great opportunities for self-financing water and sanitation projects.

Mr. OLDFIELD. Yeah. If I might add 30 seconds to that, I would ask you to consider taking a look at USAID's recent "Safeguarding the World's Water" report. I was looking at it in preparing for this hearing, looking for success stories of how water contributes to economic prosperity.

I would highlight that the partnerships office of the Development Innovation Ventures team at USAID has recently provided financial support to a group called Sanergy. It is the sort of front-end catalytic financial support that you are talking about, Mr. Blumenauer. And Sanergy then takes these funds, franchises toilets to entrepreneurs outside of Kenya who collect the waste, turn it into organic natural fertilizer, and make a profit—I think it is per toilet—of up to 2,000 U.S. a year, and several of these entrepreneurs have much more than one toilet. So it is a real business opportunity.

I would highlight USAID's SUWASA, the Sustainable Water and Sanitation in Africa Program, as well, which is not just focused on one technology or one business or financial model, but doing what it can to promote various commercial solutions and financial stability.

It is the sort of, I won't get into too much detail on this right now, but it is the sort of, I think, catalytic front-end financial and technical assistance that the U.S. taxpayer, through its trustees, through their trustees, and through USAID, should be providing. We should be first in, not last out. We should be the catalyst, not the one running around with the used drilling rig drilling wells. That is my take. I think we get a much bigger bang for the taxpayer dollar with programs like that.

Mr. BILODEAU. Yes. And briefly, I agree with Mr. Oldfield in that. USAID has led the way in terms of international financing. In our case, our entire program has cost $600 million to build. Much of that was financed by ourselves and some help from the State of California, and also we have received $20 million from the Title XVI Program.

But we provide water for 850,000 people now with our system, and so you can understand the economies of scale there and the metrics.

Mr. BLUMENAUER. Thank you. It is part of what we have attempted to do in the more recent reform legislation, is to focus on investments that the United States is involved with that are more sustainable, not using inappropriate technology or getting people started and then they don't have the wherewithal to continue with it.

Mr. Chairman, I would hope that as a result of some of this conversation there would be an opportunity to do a little deeper analysis of what we can do on the ground to help provide the foundation, because done right, it seems to me clear the evidence is that we can have programs that are actually affordable if they get over that initial hurdle in terms of understanding the technology, maybe having a little upfront financing, maybe not even grants, but financing, that there is enough money involved with some of these really in some cases tragic conditions that we could make a big difference.

Mr. ROHRABACHER. We do plan a second and probably third hearing on this issue in which we will be covering exactly the type of areas you are suggesting.

Mr. BLUMENAUER. Great. Thank you very much.

Mr. ROHRABACHER. And now we have Mr. Dan Donovan.

Mr. DONOVAN. Thank you, Mr. Chairman. I am the newest member of this committee. I have been in Congress for 4 months. I don't want you to get confused. This is my first time sitting on the upper tier. I am usually down there by where it says "staff only." So this is my first exposure——

Mr. ROHRABACHER. Don't get used to it.

Mr. DONOVAN. Thank you, Chairman.

This is my first exposure to your expertise to the probing questions of my colleagues. My understanding of the issue is just what I have read over the years. So my limited understanding and it is more general is that the problem is caused by droughts, it is caused by having adequate water but it is not safe water, there is safe water that is adequate for people but there is not infrastructure to get it to people. It is regimes or governments who have adequate water and infrastructure but won't allow their people access to it.

Are these the problems that you are facing, that these countries that you are talking about are facing, and is our country doing its share or enough to help? To anyone.

Mr. OLDFIELD. Well, thank you, Mr. Donovan. I think the easy answer to your question is yes. It is all of the above. Name a challenge associated with safe drinking water, sanitation, or hygiene, and people are facing it. Sometimes it is a lack of water.

But I guess I would quote an academic named Hans Rosling who said: The biggest environmental challenge on the planet today is that 1 billion people are drinking their neighbor's lukewarm feces. These people are not dying of thirst, they are dying of shit in the water. They are drinking each other's feces. And that is what is killing 500,000 children minimum each year.

The key, the flip side of your question is that this is solvable. The folks at this table, the folks up on the dais there understand how to solve this problem. I believe that the U.S. Government is doing a lot. I think you heard a figure of $3.5 billion for water and sanitation programs over the last 10, 12 years. That is a lot.

I personally am up here to advocate that we can do not just more, but that we can do better by addressing some of the concerns that Chairman Smith brought up earlier about how to build local capacity, how to decentralize ownership, how to make sure that we are actually working ourselves out of a job, not creating further dependencies in Africa, in Asia, and Latin America. And I would be happy in your first year here to spend some more time with you or your staff on this to bring you up to speed. And I would also direct you to Mr. Blumenauer's office and to Mr. Poe's office, who were the key sponsors of the Water for the World Act last year.

Mr. DONOVAN. Thank you.

Mr. BILODEAU. Yes. And briefly, as he mentioned, the key is that many of these areas are lacking the proper sanitation facilities. The sanitation facility is essentially the river. And if we could help developing countries develop proper sanitation facilities in concert with water reuse facilities, it solves two problems simultaneously.

Mr. WHITTINGTON. I will just tell you about a puzzle that we have in the sector. We have a lot of nonpipe technologies that work and are cheap, they are effective, and they save lives. But household demand for these services is often low. And on the other hand, household demand for pipe services, 24/7 water supply, bottled water, like you have got, is very high. But the problem is these are very expensive and they are very capital intensive.

So those are the two kind of things that we wrestle with in this sector. And it gets back to this issue of financing. How do we finance improved pipe systems for urban areas to promote growth and dynamic economies? I mean, that to me is one of the real challenges we face. We know how to save lives, and we should do it, with cheap, cost-effective technologies. But people want more than that, and they want economic growth, and they want the convenience of piped water in their homes. And so that is the challenge that we struggle with in this sector—one of the challenges we struggle with.

The other thing I would say about struggling, water problems are local and solving them requires local capacity, local institutions, and local expertise. So one of the challenges we have got is building local capacity, building local institutions, because the solutions are not the same everywhere. So it is an educational task that we have got, an institutional building task, and we all know those are really hard.

Mr. DONOVAN. I thank you all for your enlightenment.

I yield the rest of my time, Chairman.

Mr. ROHRABACHER. And last but not least, Mr. Clawson.

Mr. CLAWSON. Thank you for coming today. I have got two questions or comments that I would like you all to respond to, so I will throw them out one at a time.

So my district is—the southern tip is Marco Island. I have got the west tip of the Everglades, go up north along the coast, Naples, Bonita Springs, Fort Myers, Cabbage Key, great place. I think I have got the best district of all—wonderful, welcoming people, and I love it there. That is another conversation.

I am always concerned about diseases from mosquitos that come from water because we don't do well with drainage and pooling. And I am worried about that personally because I see chikungunya right around the corner. I see dengue fever right around the corner. It is all over the Caribbean, as far south as Brazil. And it just feels like it is knocking on our door and it is just a question of time.

And I am always worried about how we do with—you know, when I drive around my district, I am looking at a lot of pooling water and I compare that to the developing world where they don't do anything, particularly if it is a bad rainy season. And then you have 10 percent of the population of the world gets dengue fever; chikungunya is blowing up everywhere. We have this conversation today and until now I don't think anybody has even brought it up.

And I think of Southeast Asia and the rainy seasons there, and India. And, look, I am all with you on toilets and wells, but it feels like the global conversation about water sanitation and usability is behind the curve with respect to mosquitos because we beat malaria, which is a nocturnal, rural problem, and now we have chikungunya and dengue fever which is an urban, daytime problem.

So that is number one. Do we, as a country and as a globe, do we do any work on that?

The second thing is to Mr. Oldfield's comments, my experience in development in South America and Southeast Asia is that if folks are at risk a little bit, skin in the game—on the well or on the toilet, the septic system—however basic it is, that they tend to keep it up more. And that a lot of the 500,000 that are dying every year—I am a lot more open-minded to spending taxpayer money if the end user has skin in the game.

And that is not a conservative's way of saying I don't want to help, because we have all spent a big chunk of our life trying to help. But if the model makes everyone in the supply chain have skin in the game, then I think what I have seen is that we have better usage of the money.

So I would just ask you all's quick response to my two comments. First of all, if you think I am all wet on the mosquito thing, just tell me right up. And then, Mr. Oldfield, you can comment on the other one.

Mr. ROHRABACHER. I don't think all wet was what you really, wet.

Mr. WHITTINGTON. I don't think you are all wet on dengue. I think it is a serious concern. I would say that there has been rapid progress on a dengue vaccine and I would get ready to use it. You need to be ready to deploy that in your district when it is——

Mr. CLAWSON. I am really glad you—look, Dr. Whittington, if you ever have time for a conference call with my team we would love to hear it. I read a year or 2 ago that they are working on a vaccine in Singapore or in Asia somewhere. I assume it is from outside the U.S. Is that right?

Mr. WHITTINGTON. It is outside the U.S. The International Vaccine Institute in Seoul has made great progress on this and some of the pharmaceuticals. And so I would be happy to talk to you about——

Mr. CLAWSON. And does it work on all four strains of dengue fever or——

Mr. WHITTINGTON. You have got me on that. But they are very happy about the preliminary results from the trials on this. So that is something that I would get ready to use.

Mr. CLAWSON. We are very interested because we see ourselves right behind the Keys in terms of——

Mr. WHITTINGTON. I just mentioned I got back from Singapore, and they are monitoring very closely dengue cases when they pop up, they send people in to figure out where it came from, and they are really trying hard to stay on top of mosquito control. But I think your concern is exactly right. I mean, this is a real risk.

Mr. CLAWSON. Yeah. My guys tell me the type of mosquito that spreads dengue is there, but the infection is not yet in south Florida. So it just feels like a question of time before we, and I am going to be dealing with this, and if we can see it coming——

Mr. WHITTINGTON. I think you are right.

So your second point was about wells and skin in the game, and I also agree completely with you on that point, and it relates back on the other question about financing and microfinancing, getting people to pay for these services as well.

I would say that from our perspective competition in this business is useful. And one of the great advances, one of the best things that has happened in Sub-Saharan Africa in the last couple decades in the WASH sector has actually been the presence of Chinese contractors competing for contracts in the rural water sector, and they really halve the price of wells.

So the price of drilling wells, in old technology, you know, we have been having wells around for 5,000 years, but the Chinese contractors have come and competed in a market-based system for those contracts to drill wells in rural areas and have won contracts and cut the price in half. So there is a market in this business that——

——

Mr. CLAWSON. My experience in this is that when we do the financial calculation, the return, either a net present value or IRR, we leave out the cost avoidance of hepatitis C or the other things that bad toilets cause, and therefore developing countries understate the return on investment for proper sanitation. Am I right about that? Mr. Oldfield maybe?

Mr. OLDFIELD. Well, I think that is right, and I would just add time savings to that. Once you factor in the 3, 4, 6 hours a day that a lot of these women around Africa, Asia, and Latin America spend hauling water contaminated with human feces on their heads, pretty much every WASH project is financially viable. And I know that doesn't satisfy you from an NPV or an IRR perspective, but it needs to be factored in there.

Mr. CLAWSON. No, I think if you take cost avoidance in—no, I disagree. I mean, I think if you take cost avoidance in and the cost of ringworm and everything else that goes with bad water—I mean, I am conservative, but I am right with you all on that. I mean, I think the financial models, if we take all aspects into account—first of all, saving people's lives, which is always more important—then I am right with you. But I think that if we ignore the cost avoidance and if we leave the end user out of the risk stream, then we come up with corruption and other problems.

Do you agree with me on that, Mr. Oldfield?

Mr. OLDFIELD. Well, I do. I think you are on the right track here. And I am constantly looking for more ways to justify, my job is to encourage Americans, both public and private, to do more and better in tackling the world's WASH challenge, water, sanitation, and hygiene. One of our key messages is that every dollar invested in WASH provides a $4 return, according to the World Health Organization, and that $4 in return, it is not a financial return, it is barely an economic return. What it is, it is a social return.

Most of that comes from increased—well, I guess it is economic ROI—increased economic productivity because of extra hours in your day. But a significant percentage of that 4-1 ROI does come from decreased healthcare costs as well.

It is not an emerging field, but there is new research coming out on this all the time because it is, exactly as you said, it is awfully difficult to quantify precisely.

Mr. ROHRABACHER. I would like to thank our witnesses today. This is, again, a second in a series of hearings that we will have on water. And some of the areas that have been outlined by Mr. Blumenauer we are going to be looking at. And we want to—I think that we have really opened up an area of discussion on policy that could be of great value and accomplish some things in a very cost-effective way.

So I want to thank you for helping start this dialogue on water, and we will continue in the next hearing, but this one is adjourned.

[Whereupon, at 3:20 p.m., the subcommittees were adjourned.]

APPENDIX

MATERIAL SUBMITTED FOR THE RECORD

JOINT SUBCOMMITTEE HEARING NOTICE
COMMITTEE ON FOREIGN AFFAIRS
U.S. HOUSE OF REPRESENTATIVES
WASHINGTON, D.C. 20515-6128

Subcommittee on Europe, Eurasia, and Emerging Threats
Dana Rohrabacher (R-CA), Chairman

Subcommittee on Africa, Global Health, Global Human Rights, and International Organizations
Christopher H. Smith (R-NJ), Chairman

September 2, 2015

TO: MEMBERS OF THE COMMITTEE ON FOREIGN AFFAIRS

You are respectfully requested to attend an OPEN hearing of the Committee on Foreign Affairs, to be held jointly by the Subcommittee on Europe, Eurasia, and Emerging Threats, and the Subcommittee on Africa, Global Health, Global Human Rights, and International Organizations in Room 2172 of the Rayburn House Office Building (and available on the Committee website at www.foreignaffairs.gov):

DATE: Wednesday, September 9, 2015

TIME: 2:00 p.m.

SUBJECT: The Role of Water in Avoiding Conflict and Building Prosperity

WITNESSES: Mr. John Oldfield
                   Chief Executive Officer
                   WASH Advocates

                   Mr. Denis Bilodeau
                   1st Vice President
                   Orange County Water District Board of Directors

                   Dale Whittington, Ph.D
                   Professor
                   University of North Carolina

By Direction of the Chairman

COMMITTEE ON FOREIGN AFFAIRS

MINUTES OF SUBCOMMITTEE ON _Europe, Eurasia, and Emerging Threats/Africa, Global Health, Global Human Rights, and International Organizations_ HEARING

Day __*Wednesday*__ Date __*September 9, 2015*__ Room _____*2172*_____

Starting Time __*2:07 pm*__ Ending Time __*3:20 pm*__

Recesses __*0*__ (____to____) (____to____) (____to____) (____to____) (____to____) (____to____)

Presiding Member(s)

Rep. Rohrabacher, Rep. Smith

Check all of the following that apply:

Open Session ☑
Executive (closed) Session ☐
Televised ☐

Electronically Recorded (taped) ☑
Stenographic Record ☑

TITLE OF HEARING:

The Role of Water in Avoiding Conflict and Building Prosperity

---

SUBCOMMITTEE MEMBERS PRESENT:

Rep. Clawson, Rep. Donovan, Rep. Rohrabacher, Rep. Smith

NON-SUBCOMMITTEE MEMBERS PRESENT: *(Mark with an * if they are not members of full committee.)*

*Rep. Blumenauer

HEARING WITNESSES: Same as meeting notice attached? Yes ☑ **No** ☐
(If "no", please list below and include title, agency, department, or organization.)

STATEMENTS FOR THE RECORD: *(List any statements submitted for the record.)*

TIME SCHEDULED TO RECONVENE _____
or
TIME ADJOURNED __*3:20 pm*__

Subcommittee Staff Director

www.ingramcontent.com/pod-product-compliance
Lightning Source LLC
Chambersburg PA
CBHW081114280526
45787CB00007B/2832